RAILS FROM SHREWSBURY

A PICTORIAL JOURNEY, 1970s-2012

PETER J. GREEN

PEN & SWORD TRANSPORT

AN IMPRINT OF PEN & SWORD BOOKS LTD.
YORKSHIRE – PHILADELPHIA

First published in Great Britain in 2023 by
Pen and Sword Transport
An imprint of
Pen & Sword Books Ltd.
Yorkshire - Philadelphia

Copyright © Peter J. Green, 2023

ISBN 978 1 39904 269 7

The right of Peter J. Green to be identified as author of this work has been asserted by him in accordance with the Copyright, Designs and Patents Act 1988.

A CIP catalogue record for this book is available from the British Library.

All rights reserved. No part of this book may be reproduced or transmitted in any form or by any means, electronic or mechanical including photocopying, recording or by any information storage and retrieval system, without permission from the Publisher in writing.

Typeset by SJmagic DESIGN SERVICES, India.

Printed and bound in the UK by CPI Group (UK) Ltd., Croydon. CR0 4YY.

Pen & Sword Books Ltd incorporates the imprints of Pen & Sword Books Archaeology, Atlas, Aviation, Battleground, Discovery, Family History, History, Maritime, Military, Naval, Politics, Railways, Select, Transport, True Crime, Fiction, Frontline Books, Leo Cooper, Praetorian Press, Seaforth Publishing, Wharncliffe and White Owl.

For a complete list of Pen & Sword titles please contact

PEN & SWORD BOOKS LIMITED
47 Church Street, Barnsley, South Yorkshire, S70 2AS, England
E-mail: enquiries@pen-and-sword.co.uk
Website: www.pen-and-sword.co.uk

or

PEN AND SWORD BOOKS
1950 Lawrence Rd, Havertown, PA 19083, USA
E-mail: Uspen-and-sword@casematepublishers.com
Website: www.penandswordbooks.com

CONTENTS

Introduction 7

Acknowledgements 9

Map of lines from Shrewsbury 10

Around Shrewsbury Station .... Photos 1-21

Shrewsbury to Gobowen .... Photos 22-36

Gobowen to Blodwell Quarry .... Photos 37-42

Gobowen to Wrexham General .... Photos 43-57

Wrexham Central to Hawarden Bridge .... Photos 58-63

Wrexham General to Chester .... Photos 64-73

Shrewsbury to Crewe .... Photos 74-105

Shrewsbury to Wellington .... Photos 106-123

Wellington to Donnington .... Photos 124-128

Wellington to Madeley Junction .... Photos 129-130

Madeley Junction to Ironbridge .... Photos 131-137

Madeley Junction to Wolverhampton .... Photos 138-152

Shrewsbury to Abbey .... Photos 153-154

Shrewsbury to Welshpool .... Photos 155-169

Shrewsbury to Craven Arms .... Photos 170-196

Craven Arms to Knighton .... Photos 197-204

Craven Arms to Hereford .... Photos 205-234

Steam-hauled special trains .... Photos 235-250

The Llangollen Railway .... Photos 251-252

The Telford Steam Railway .... Photos 253-254

The Severn Valley Railway .... Photos 255-263

The Welshpool and Llanfair Light Railway .... Photos 264-265

Other Recent Preservation Projects .... Photos 266-268

Bibliography 202

Index to Locations by Photo Number 203

INTRODUCTION

This book is a photographic record of the railways of Shrewsbury and the lines radiating from there, commencing in 1974 and ending in 2012, with the majority of the photographs dating from the 1980s and 1990s. To help to complete the story, a few more recent photographs are included.

My earliest interest in railways was collecting locomotive numbers, which were duly crossed off in my Ian Allan Locospotters' books. My father was a keen photographer and, encouraged by him, I soon began taking photographs of my favourite locomotives. He was also a very enthusiastic gardener and liked to visit the Shrewsbury Flower Show each year. On a number of occasions, I went with him on these visits. It then occurred to me that it would be good to spend a day at Shrewsbury railway station, so, one day in the early 1960s, we set off in the family car to Shrewsbury where I and a trainspotter friend of mine were duly deposited at the railway station for the day. This was to be the first of the many visits I was to make to Shrewsbury for its railways. My memories of the day include seeing Manor class 4-6-0 locomotives from Aberystwyth with the hinges of their smokebox doors painted white. One surprising sighting was Coronation class 4-6-2 46239 *City of Chester*, in filthy condition, perhaps en route to Crewe Works. Unfortunately, it was not a 'cop'.

It was not until the 1970s when I again visited Shrewsbury for its railways. The attraction at that time was the frequent steam-hauled special trains that ran on the Welsh Marches line between Newport and Chester. A few photos of them are included here. Of course, diesels were photographed as well, as time permitted.

As my interest in photographing the modern scene increased in the early 1980s, I began to visit Shrewsbury much more frequently, anxious to capture a fascinating railway centre on film before things changed too much. Lines from Chester, Crewe, Wolverhampton and Hereford converged at Shrewsbury, so there was no shortage of activity and a good variety of motive power. For those interested in signalling, the area retained a mixture of upper and lower quadrant signals controlled from signal boxes of various designs, some of which still remain today.

Each of the lines which joined at Shrewsbury had its own character and all featured semaphore signalling. In addition, the LNWR/GWR line, leading to the former Cambrian line, diverged from the Hereford line at Sutton Bridge Junction, Shrewsbury, the Central Wales line headed into Wales at Craven Arms, and the Bidston line ran north from Wrexham. These lines are included as far as Welshpool, Knighton and Hawarden Bridge. Former passenger lines, by then used only for freight traffic, also feature, including the Blodwell Quarry line from Gobowen, the Donnington line from Wellington, and the line to Ironbridge Power Station from Madeley Junction, near Telford.

Class 37 diesel-electric locomotives took over services on the former Cambrian line to Aberystwyth and Pwllheli in the 1980s and soon became a common sight on passenger trains to Wolverhampton, and on the Welsh Marches line. This increased the appeal of the area even more for me, the class being a particular favourite of mine. Other types, including classes 25, 31, 33, and 47, also frequently appeared.

A short section, showing something of the heritage railways in the area, is also included here.

Peter J. Green
Worcester, England
2022

ACKNOWLEDGEMENTS

Paul Dorney, Steve Turner and David Rostance have each contributed to this book, both with photographs and additional information, which has helped me to make it more complete. They have also assisted by identifying a number of errors that I made.

James Billingham, who accompanied me on many of my visits, has also helped with information. My recording of the details of diesel multiple unit workings was not as good as it should have been in the 1980s. Fortunately he has been able to help me with this, as well as suggesting other additions and corrections to this work.

Val Brown has, once again, checked the text and corrected the many mistakes I have made.

My thanks go to you all.

Peter J. Green

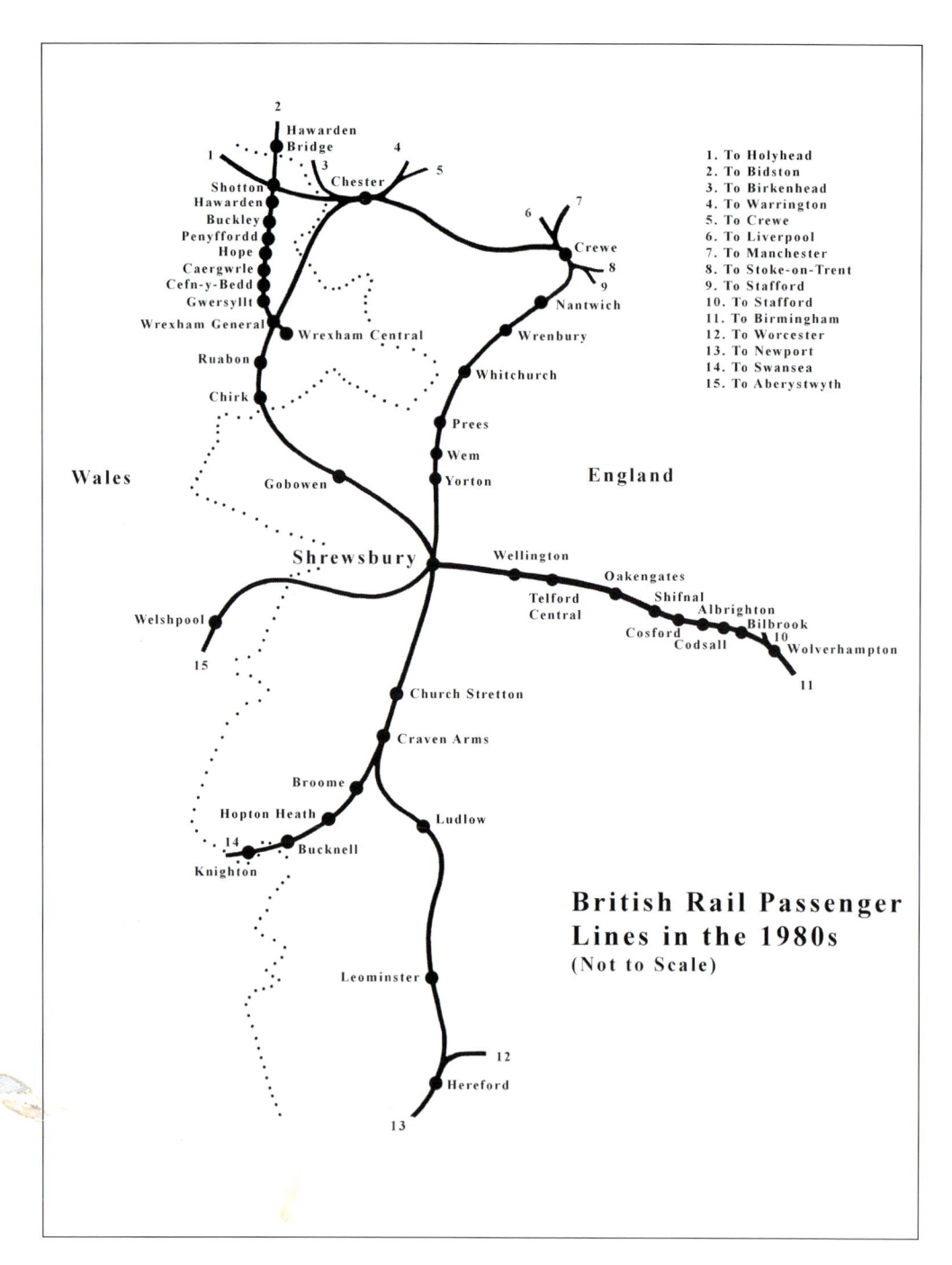

Map of the British Rail passenger lines radiating from Shrewsbury. For clarity, freight lines and preserved railways have not been included.

AROUND SHREWSBURY STATION

1. **Operated jointly** by the Great Western Railway and the London and North Western Railway, Shrewsbury railway station, originally known as Shrewsbury General, was built in 1848 by Thomas Mainwaring Penson of Oswestry. Between 1899 and 1903, the station was extended by constructing a new floor underneath the original building. Shrewsbury Castle, dating from 1070, is just to the south of the station building. 27 January 2022.

2. Built in imitation Tudor style, Shrewsbury station building has carvings of Tudor-style heads around its window frames. It is a Grade II listed building. 27 January 2022.

Opposite above: **3. Shrewsbury station** had seven platforms, but platforms 1 and 2 have been out of use since the 1980s. Here, English Electric class 37/7 37895 heads a northbound permanent way train through the station, between platforms 3 and 4. Shrewsbury Abbey is in the background. 19 December 1987.

Opposite below: **4. Brush class 47/4** 47529 arrives at Shrewsbury with the 13.45 Manchester Piccadilly to Cardiff Central. Class 150 Sprinter 150 138 is stabled in platform 3. 30 December 1986.

AROUND SHREWSBURY STATION • **13**

14 • RAILS FROM SHREWSBURY

5. Looking north at Shrewsbury station, Sulzer class 25/2 25119 stands in platform 7 with a parcels train. Metro-Cammell class 101 diesel multiple unit (DMU) set C802 is in platform 6, while a class 116 DMU waits for its departure time to Wolverhampton in platform 5. 31 August 1983.

Opposite above: **6. A class 120 DMU** stands in platform 4, as class 25/3 diesel-electric 25251 and class 25/2 25237 head through the middle road towards Coton Hill with a northbound tank train. 31 August 1983.

Opposite below: **7. With Laura's** Tower in the background, Sulzer class 25/2 25201 rests between duties next to the former platform 2 at Shrewsbury station. 30 December 1986.

AROUND SHREWSBURY STATION • 15

8. Shrewsbury station's platforms extend over the River Severn. Here, class 25/2 25245 heads a short parcels train away from the station and across the bridge over the river. Shrewsbury Prison is in the background. 31 August 1983.

Opposite above: **9. After arriving** with a train from London Euston, class 47/4 47645 *Robert F. Fairlie Locomotive Engineer 1831-1885* stands at the south end of platform 7 at Shrewsbury railway station. Severn Bridge Junction signal box is in the background. Note the centre-pivot signals on the end of the platform. 30 December 1986.

Opposite below: **10. With Shrewsbury** Abbey in the background, a Metro-Cammell class 101 DMU, forming a Shrewsbury to Aberystwyth service, passes Severn Bridge Junction signal box as it departs from Shrewsbury. Built in 1902 to an earlier London and North Western Railway (LNWR) design and containing a 180 lever frame, the signal box is now the largest operational mechanical signal box in the world, following the closure of a signal box in Australia in 2011. Renovated in 2021, it is a Grade II listed building. 30 December 1986.

AROUND SHREWSBURY STATION • 17

11. Class 150 Sprinter 150 120 and a second unidentified unit, forming a Wolverhampton to Shrewsbury service, passes a Royal Mail Letters coach, as it approaches its destination. 19 December 1987.

Opposite above: **12. After passing** platform 7 at Shrewsbury station, class 37/7 37800 *Glo Cymru* takes the line to Sutton Bridge Junction with a train of empty Cawoods coal containers from Ellesmere Port to Abercwmboi. Class 37/4 37429 *Eisteddfod Genedlaethol* is on the left. 19 December 1987.

Opposite below: **13. Class 150** Sprinter 150 148 with a second unidentified unit behind, forming a service to Wolverhampton, departs from one of the bay platforms at Shrewsbury station. 19 December 1987.

AROUND SHREWSBURY STATION • **19**

14. This is the view of Severn Bridge Junction, the junction of the Wolverhampton line and the line to Sutton Bridge Junction and Hereford, as seen from Shrewsbury Castle. On the left, beyond the stabled DMUs, class 47/4 47540 waits for the road into the station with a train from London Euston. Class 37/0 diesel-electrics 37176 and 37147 are preparing to take over a Cambrian line train, and on the right, class 47/0 47245 is arriving at platform 4 with a Cardiff Central to Crewe service. The station avoiding line, used to turn locomotives in steam days, can be seen behind the signal box. 7 September 1985.

Opposite above: **15. With work** proceeding on Shrewsbury Abbey in the background, class 37/4 37428 *David Lloyd George* arrives at Shrewsbury's platform 4 with the 1M84 10.45 Cardiff Central to Crewe. 19 December 1987.

Opposite below: **16. After arriving** at Shrewsbury with a service from London Euston, class 47/4 47454 has run off its train onto the Crewe line at Crewe Junction, at the north end of the station, prior to running round. 31 August 1983.

AROUND SHREWSBURY STATION • 21

17. The lines to Chester, on the left, and Crewe divide at Crewe Junction. Here, class 150 Sprinter 150 145, forming a Chester to Shrewsbury service, approaches Shrewsbury station. The bridge behind the signal gantry is to facilitate the movement of parcels etc. 19 December 1987.

Opposite above: **18. Class 150 Sprinter** 150 106 shunts past Crewe Junction signal box at the north end of Shrewsbury station. The impressive box was built in 1903 to an LNWR design and houses a 120 lever interlocking frame. It is much taller than it appears here since its base is at ground level and the railway is on a viaduct. The lines on the left lead to Crewe. 25 August 1986.

Opposite below: **19. Class 37/4** 37426 *Y Lein Fach/Vale of Rheidol* takes the line to Crewe at Crewe Junction as it heads the 1M84 10.45 Cardiff Central to Crewe away from Shrewsbury. 13 February 1988.

AROUND SHREWSBURY STATION • **23**

20. With Shrewsbury Castle in the background, class 47/4 47453 rounds the curve at Crewe Junction with the 14.15 Cardiff Central to Holyhead. 26 July 1986.

21. A three-car DMU, a class 116/115 hybrid, shunts past Crewe Junction signal box and onto the Crewe line at Shrewsbury. It was common at this time for DMU formations to include a centre car from a different class of DMU. In this case, the class 116 DMU is running with the centre car from a class 115 unit. 30 December 1986.

SHREWSBURY TO GOBOWEN

22. **Class 31/1** 31121 heads a permanent way train from the Chester line past Castle Foregate goods shed and towards Shrewsbury station. Coton Hill Yard is just beyond the road bridge in the background. 19 December 1987.

23. With a fogman's hut on the left, class 150 Sprinter 150 111, forming the 07.54 Wolverhampton to Chester, departs from Shrewsbury and approaches Coton Hill. The line on the left leads to Coton Hill Yard. 29 July 1989.

Opposite above: **24. Class 150 Sprinter** 150 117, forming a Chester to Shrewsbury service, approaches Shrewsbury station. The goods shed behind the train was built in 1848 as a locomotive depot by the Shrewsbury and Chester Railway (S&CR). It was absorbed by the Great Western Railway (GWR) in 1854 and became Coton Hill South, closing in 1883. 16 August 1986.

Opposite below: **25. After running** through Shrewsbury station, class 08 diesel-electric shunter 08585 takes the line to Coton Hill Yard with a trip freight from Shrewsbury Abbey. The oil tanks, which originated at Bromford Bridge, arrived at Coton Hill on the 7J36 Speedlink service from Bescot. On the left is the goods shed at Castle Foregate. The shed now houses a number of small businesses. 10 September 1987.

SHREWSBURY TO GOBOWEN • **27**

26. Still with a Welsh Highland Terrier emblem on its bodyside, former Eastfield class 47/0 47120 heads out of Coton Hill Yard with the 7G19 Speedlink service to Bescot, including tanks from Esso at Abbey. A class 08 shunter stands in the yard. 22 February 1988. *(Paul Dorney Photo)*

Opposite above: **27. An open** day was held at Coton Hill Yard in 1993, at the same time as an open day at Hereford. Regional Railways ran various special trains between the locations, as well as to other destinations, using a variety of motive power. Prominent in Coton Hill Yard is class 31/1 31141 carrying a 'Cambrian Limited' headboard. The nameplate is covered but the locomotive was named *Floreat Salopia* later in the day. Other exhibits include class 37s, a Deltic, a class 58, and a class 86 electric. 30 May 1993.

Opposite below: **28. Class 150 Sprinter** 150 110, forming a Chester to Shrewsbury service, passes Coton Hill Yard. 28 March 1987.

SHREWSBURY TO GOBOWEN • 29

29. Class 31/1 31287 heads south at Leaton with a loaded stone train from Blodwell Quarry to Bescot. Opened in 1848 by the S&CR, Leaton station was rebuilt by the GWR around 1900. It was closed to passengers in 1960, closing completely in 1965. The original signal box was replaced in 1905 by a GWR Type 27c box with a 21 lever frame. The box closed in 1988 and was moved to Glyndyfrdwy on the Llangollen Railway. 13 August 1987.

Opposite above: **30. Baschurch signal** box stands next to the level crossing on Station Road. A McKenzie and Holland Type 3 box, it was built in 1880 for the GWR and housed a 25 lever frame, dating from 1911. The box was closed in March 1999 and is a Grade II listed building. 1 August 1986. *(Paul Dorney Photo)*

Opposite below: **31. Haughton Sidings** signal box, located between Baschurch and Whittington, was a GWR Type 7a box with a 29 lever frame. The box closed in 1991 when the loop was removed. 4 August 1987. *(Paul Dorney Photo)*

SHREWSBURY TO GOBOWEN • 31

32. An unidentified class 47 heads past Haughton Sidings with a Margam to Dee Marsh loaded steel train. Haughton Sidings signal box is beyond the bridge. 10 August 1983. *(Paul Dorney Photo)*

SHREWSBURY TO GOBOWEN • **33**

33. Whittington Low Level station was opened by the S&CR as Whittington in 1848. In 1864, the Cambrian Railway (CR) opened a station at Whittington on their Oswestry to Ellesmere line a short distance to the north. In 1924, the station was renamed Whittington Low Level and the former CR station became Whittington High Level. The Low Level station closed to all traffic in 1963. The GWR Whittington Low Level signal box, a McKenzie & Holland Type 3 design opened in 1881, was closed in 1992. 4 August 1987. *(Paul Dorney Photo)*

34. A two-car class 116 DMU, forming the 14.21 Chester to Shrewsbury service, approaches the GWR Gobowen South signal box. The box was located at the junction of the lines to Oswestry and Shrewsbury. A McKenzie and Holland type 3 design, it opened in the early 1880s. The box was closed less than a week after this photograph was taken. 30 May 1987.

Opposite above: **35. After arriving** with the 6J43 13.35 Washwood Heath Up Sidings loaded coal train, class 37/5 37693 stands in a disused platform at Gobowen. The station was opened in 1848 by the S&CR. It was built in an Italianate style and is a Grade II listed building. Gobowen was previously the junction station for Oswestry, around three miles away. 23 July 1987.

Opposite below: **36. The driver** of class 37/0 37235 turns on the power as it heads away from Gobowen with two empty coal wagons. The working is the 6G26 18.30 Gobowen to Washwood Heath Up Sidings. 10 September 1987.

SHREWSBURY TO GOBOWEN • 35

GOBOWEN TO BLODWELL QUARRY

37. After running round its train at Gobowen, class 31/1 31124 heads the 7J02 09.58 Bescot Up Yard to Blodwell Quarry empty stone train past Oswestry station building, the former headquarters of the Cambrian Railway. Locomotives and stock of the Cambrian Heritage Railways are on the left. Based at Oswestry and Llynclys, the organisation is working to reopen the line which was mothballed after the Blodwell Quarry trains ceased in 1988. 10 September 1987.

Opposite above: **38. Class 31/1** 31230 passes Oswestry station with an empty stone train to Blodwell Quarry. Oswestry South signal box is a Dutton Type 2 design, opened in 1892. The box, closed in 1970, has since been restored. 16 June 1988.

Opposite below: **39. Class 31/1** 31287 runs through the closed Oswestry station, as it heads north to Gobowen with the 7G25 15.21 Blodwell Quarry to Bescot Up Yard loaded stone train. 13 August 1987.

GOBOWEN TO BLODWELL QUARRY • 37

40. Class 31/1 31230 is pictured running down the branch near Blodwell Quarry with an empty stone train. 16 June 1988.

41. Class 31/1 31124 waits to cross the A495 road between Llynclys and Porthywaen at the closed Porthywaen station, with an empty stone train from Bescot to Blodwell Quarry. 10 September 1987.

GOBOWEN TO BLODWELL QUARRY • 39

42. After arriving with a train from Bescot, class 31/1 31124 stands at the ARC Blodwell Quarry, near Llanyblodwel. 10 September 1987.

GOBOWEN TO WREXHAM GENERAL

Above: **43. A DMU,** made up of a class 108 two-car set and an unidentified three-car set, forming a Chester to Shrewsbury service, approaches Gobowen station. The GWR Gobowen North signal box is a Mckenzie and Holland design dating from 1884, containing a 16 lever frame. 1 March 1986.

Opposite above: **44. Class 37/9** 37905 *Vulcan Enterprise* approaches Gobowen with a Dee Marsh to Llanwern steel train. Comparing this photo with the previous one taken sixteen months earlier, the telegraph poles have gone, as has the distant signal following the closure of Gobowen South signal box, and the signal box has been fitted with modern window frames. 23 July 1987.

Below: **45. In February** 1995, Hertfordshire Rail Tours ran 'The Whistle Test' railtour from London Waterloo to Chester and Crewe. Motive power was provided by class 33/0 locomotives 33065 *Sealion* and 33063 throughout. Here, the train is pictured heading north from Gobowen, en route to Chester. 25 February 1995.

46. Class 47/4 47663 heads a diverted Liverpool Lime Street to Southampton service past Weston Rhyn. 13 November 1988.

Opposite above: **47. A class 116 DMU,** forming the 12.47 Shrewsbury to Chester service, approaches the level crossing at Weston Rhyn. Weston Rhyn station was previously named Preesgweene and was renamed in 1935. It was closed in 1960 and is now a private residence. The Mckenzie and Holland signal box was opened in 1880 by the GWR and was rebuilt in 1924, when it was fitted with a GWR type 28b timber top. After closure in 1991, the signal box was moved to the Llangollen Railway where it is now sited at Corwen. 30 May 1987.

Opposite below: **48. Class 47/4** 47647 crosses Chirk Viaduct with the diverted 1V55 12.25 Preston to Bristol Temple Meads. Built in 1848, Chirk Viaduct carries the Shrewsbury to Chester railway across the Ceiriog Valley. The viaduct is approximately 849ft long with sixteen arches. Behind the railway viaduct is Chirk Aqueduct, built in 1801. It is 710ft long with ten arches and carries the Llangollen Canal across the valley. 13 November 1988.

GOBOWEN TO WREXHAM GENERAL • 43

44 • RAILS FROM SHREWSBURY

49. Two class 37 diesel-electrics head south across Chirk Viaduct over the River Ceiriog. Chirk Aqueduct, carrying the Llangollen Canal, is on the left. 4 March 1989.

Opposite above: **50. To the** south of Ruabon, the nineteen-arch Cefn Mawr Viaduct crosses the River Dee. The viaduct, built in 1848, is a Grade II listed structure. Here, a class 116 two-car DMU, forming a Chester to Wolverhampton service, heads south over the viaduct. 30 May 1987.

Opposite below: **51. Class 150 Sprinter** 150 133, forming the 10.47 Shrewsbury to Chester service, passes the signal box as it approaches Ruabon station. The box, boarded-up and switched out, is the former GWR Ruabon Middle signal box. 30 May 1987.

GOBOWEN TO WREXHAM GENERAL • 45

52. A class 120 DMU pauses at Ruabon before heading north to Chester. Ruabon station was opened in 1846 on the Shrewsbury to Chester line, later part of the GWR route from London Paddington to Birkenhead. It was also the terminus of the Ruabon to Barmouth line, closed in 1968. 8 April 1978.

Opposite above: **53. By 1987,** the canopies had been removed from both platforms at Ruabon station. Here, a Metro-Cammell class 101 DMU, forming the 17.38 Chester to Shrewsbury service, arrives at Ruabon. 30 May 1987.

Opposite below: **54. Class 150 Sprinter** 150 137, forming a Shrewsbury to Chester service, passes Bersham Colliery, near Rhostyllen. The colliery closed in December 1986. Bersham Sidings signal box, in the background, was closed in February 1987. 11 April 1987.

GOBOWEN TO WREXHAM GENERAL • 47

55. With Croes Newydd North Fork signal box in the background, class 37/0 37274, in Mainline livery, heads south from Wrexham with the 6J70 Warrington Arpley to Chirk Kronospan timber train. On the left is the site of the former Croes Newydd locomotive depot. 11 March 1998. *(Paul Dorney Photo)*

Opposite above: **56. British Rail** class 56 56134 *Blyth Power* passes Wrexham General station with the 6S75 Dee Marsh to Mossend empty timber train. Croes Newydd North Fork signal box is in the background. The signal box, a GWR type 27c design fitted with a 45 lever frame, opened around 1906. In 1940, it was extended to accommodate an 83 lever frame. In 2009, the frame was removed and a signalling panel was installed. 11 March 1998. *(Paul Dorney Photo)*

Opposite below: **57. Class 47/0** 47206 heads north through Wrexham General station with a freight to Arpley Sidings, Warrington. 12 June 1991. *(Paul Dorney Photo)*

GOBOWEN TO WREXHAM GENERAL • 49

WREXHAM CENTRAL TO HAWARDEN BRIDGE

Above: **58. Wrexham Central** station is the southern terminus of the Wrexham to Bidston line. The current station opened in 1998 in Wrexham town centre, replacing an earlier station dating from 1887. Here, refurbished class 37 locomotive 97303 stands in the platform with the 1Q09 09.35 Shrewsbury Abbey Foregate Carriage Sidings to Longsight test train, with 97304 on the rear. St Giles' church is in the background. 4 August 2011. *(Steve Turner Photo)*

Opposite above: **59. After arriving** from Wrexham Central, Class 142 Pacer 142 031, forming a Bidston service, waits at Wrexham General platform 4. This part of the station was originally Wrexham Exchange station. The old station building, since demolished, is on the right. 25 January 1986.

Opposite below: **60. Class 56** 56087 *ABP Port of Hull* is pictured near Cefn-y-Bedd, north of Wrexham, with the 6M84 Margam to Dee Marsh steel coils. 25 February 1998. *(Paul Dorney Photo)*

WREXHAM CENTRAL TO HAWARDEN BRIDGE • 51

52 • RAILS FROM SHREWSBURY

61. Class 142 Pacer 142 052, forming the 2J73 13.32 Bidston to Wrexham Central, arrives at Penyffordd. The signal box is a British Railways (London Midland Region) type 15 design, built in 1972. 16 July 1994. *(Steve Turner Photo)*

Opposite above: **62. Class 56** 56040 *Oystermouth* heads the 6V78 15.30 Dee Marsh Junction to Margam Yard away from Shotton High Level station. There is also a Shotton Low Level station, located on the North Wales Coast line. 3 September 1994. *(Steve Turner Photo)*

Opposite below: **63. In heavy** rain, class 60 60057 *Adam Smith* exits the bridge over the River Dee and approaches Hawarden Bridge station with the 6M64 17.10 Elgin to Dee Marsh Junction timber train. 3 September 1994. *(Steve Turner Photo)*

WREXHAM CENTRAL TO HAWARDEN BRIDGE • **53**

WREXHAM GENERAL TO CHESTER

Above: **64. British Rail** class 56 56105 is pictured at Wrexham General with the 6S75 Dee Marsh to Mossend timber train. The line on the left is the former Great Central Railway (GCR) line from Wrexham Central to Bidston. The lines on the right are the GWR lines to Chester. 11 February 1998. *(Paul Dorney Photo)*

Opposite above: **65. Class 33/0** 'Cromptons' 33051 *Shakespeare Cliff* and 33030 head Pathfinder Tours' 'The Crompton Culminator' north, near Rossett, on the single line between Wrexham and Saltney Junction, Chester. The special train ran from Salisbury to Holyhead with the 'Cromptons' heading the train from Bristol Temple Meads to Holyhead and back. 6 September 1997.

WREXHAM GENERAL TO CHESTER • **55**

Below: **66. Rossett station,** located about six miles north of Wrexham, was opened in 1846. It closed to passengers in 1964 and to freight in 1968. Here, a class 101 DMU heads south to Shrewsbury, past Rossett signal box, while class 37/0 37117 waits at the crossing with a short permanent way train. The signal box, a British Railways (Western Region) Type 37a box with a 40 lever frame, was opened in 1960, replacing two earlier boxes. Just over a week after this photo was taken, the line through Rossett was singled and the signal box was closed. 25 January 1986.

56 • RAILS FROM SHREWSBURY

67. At Saltney Junction, near Chester, the line from Shrewsbury joins the North Wales Coast line from Holyhead. Here, class 47/4 47509 *Albion,* in InterCity livery, heads the 09.07 Holyhead to London Euston past the junction. Note the Driving Van Trailer (DVT) behind the locomotive. At Crewe, an electric locomotive will be attached to the other end of the train for the journey to London. 21 September 1991.

Opposite above: **68. Class 20** diesel-electrics 20151 and 20059 lead an empty coal train, from Fiddlers Ferry Power Station at Warrington to Point of Ayr Colliery, across the River Dee Bridge at Chester. Chester Racecourse is on the right. 31 August 1991.

Opposite below: **69. Class 37/4** 37425 *Sir Robert McAlpine/Concrete Bob* passes Northgate Locks, on the Shropshire Union Canal Main Line, as it heads the 09.32 Crewe to Holyhead away from Chester. The spire of Northgate Church is in the background. 29 April 1995.

WREXHAM GENERAL TO CHESTER • 57

70. Class 40 40150 heads the 1D40 14.36 Manchester Victoria to Llandudno away from Chester. The train is passing under Chester No. 6 signal box, a type 4 box built by the LNWR in 1903 and fitted with an 80 lever frame. It was closed in 1984 during the Chester resignalling. 31 July 1983.

Opposite above: **71. Class 37/4** 37407 *Blackpool Tower* approaches Chester station with the 14.53 Holyhead to Crewe. The line to Birkenhead curves away to the right behind the far shed, while the front of a class 73 can be seen in the former GWR locomotive shed on the right. 3 June 1995.

Opposite below: **72. Before resignalling,** class 47/4 47463 heads the diverted 1A07 07.37 Liverpool Lime Street to London Euston past Chester No. 2 signal box as it departs from Chester. The Italianate style Chester station was opened in 1848 and was progressively extended over the next forty years. The station has seven platforms and is a Grade II listed building. The LNWR type 4 signal box was closed in 1984. 31 July 1983.

WREXHAM GENERAL TO CHESTER • 59

73. After resignalling and the removal of Chester No. 2 signal box, Chester station is more clearly visible. Here, class 37/4 37422 *Robert F. Fairlie* departs from Chester with the 11.22 Bangor to Crewe. 8 February 1997.

SHREWSBURY TO CREWE

74. Class 37/0 37139 heads the 1M74 13.30 Cardiff Central to Liverpool Lime Street away from Crewe Junction, Shrewsbury. 8 September 1990.

75. Class 108 DMU set S944, forming a Crewe to Swansea service via the Central Wales Line, approaches Crewe Junction, Shrewsbury. Note the mixture of upper and lower quadrant signals. 30 January 1988.

Opposite above: **76. A three-car** class 116/115 hybrid DMU, forming a Crewe to Shrewsbury service, passes Crewe Bank signal box and approaches Crewe Junction, as it heads for Shrewsbury station. 26 July 1986.

Opposite below: **77. After arriving** at Shrewsbury with a train from London Euston, class 31/4 diesel-electrics 31405 and 31412 head the empty stock to Crewe Bank, where the locomotives will run round their train. Note the equipment of J. A. Smallshaw coal merchants on the right. 30 January 1988.

SHREWSBURY TO CREWE • **63**

78. Class 47/3 47356 passes Shrewsbury Crewe Bank with the 3V20 15.10 Manchester to Bristol Temple Meads parcels. In 1986, parcels trains were transferred from the parcels depot at the former Mayfield station to Manchester Piccadilly. 26 July 1986.

Opposite above: **79. Class 47/4** 47531 heads north at Shrewsbury Crewe Bank with the 1M70 07.50 Swansea to Manchester Piccadilly. The lines on the right lead to Castle Foregate Goods and the premises of J. A. Smallshaw coal merchants. 2 August 1986.

Opposite below: **80. The railway** from Shrewsbury to Crewe was opened in 1858, becoming part of the London Midland and Scottish Railway (LMSR) in 1923. Here, class 150 Sprinter 150 110, forming a Crewe to Shrewsbury service, approaches Crewe Bank signal box. The box is a LMSR type 13 design dating from 1943, fitted with a 45 lever frame. It closed in 2013 when the line was resignalled. 3 January 1987.

SHREWSBURY TO CREWE • 65

81. Class 66 66247 stands with a coal train from Arpley Sidings, Warrington, at Smallshaw's coal merchants at Castle Foregate, Shrewsbury. 15 February 2001. *(Paul Dorney Photo)*

Opposite above: **82. Class 37/4** 37407 *Loch Long* is pictured with the 1V08 09.15 Liverpool Lime Street to Cardiff Central, between Harlescott Crossing and Shrewsbury Crewe Bank, as it heads for Shrewsbury station. 4 March 1989.

Opposite below: **83. Harlescott Crossing** signal box, located on the edge of Shrewsbury, is a London and North Western Railway (LNWR) design fitted with a 38 lever frame, built in 1882. It closed in 2013. 30 January 1988.

SHREWSBURY TO CREWE • **67**

84. Class 47/4 47466 heads the 07.45 Swansea to Manchester Piccadilly through Yorton station. The station, located seven miles north of Shrewsbury, opened in 1858. 22 August 1987.

Opposite above: **85. On what** was usually a class 25 diagram, class 46 46014 passes Yorton station with the 10.00 Crewe to Cardiff Central. 18 April 1981. *(David Rostance Photo)*

Opposite below: **86. Class 156 Sprinter** 156 461, forming the 08.08 Cardiff Central to Manchester Piccadilly, approaches Wem. 13 May 1989.

SHREWSBURY TO CREWE • 69

87. **Class 37/0** 37250 and class 37/4 37427 *Bont Y Bermo* pass Wem station with the 3V20 15.10 Manchester Piccadilly to Bristol Temple Meads parcels. The station, eleven miles north of Shrewsbury on the line to Crewe, opened in 1858. 15 August 1987.

Opposite above: 88. **Class 37/9** 37905 *Vulcan Enterprise* runs through Wem station with a southbound steel train. 13 May 1989.

Opposite below: 89. **Class 101 Metro-Cammell** DMU set S800 and a second two-car unit, forming a Crewe to Swansea service, arrive at Wem. The LNWR type 4 signal box, opened around 1882, was closed in 2013 and demolished two years later. 15 August 1987.

SHREWSBURY TO CREWE • 71

90. Class 47/4 47557 approaches Prees with the 07.45 Swansea to Manchester Piccadilly. Opened in 1881, Prees signal box is a LNWR type 4 design, fitted with a 25 lever frame. It closed in 2013. Prees station was opened by the Crewe and Shrewsbury Railway in 1858. 15 August 1987.

Opposite above: **91. Class 33/0** 33017 departs from Whitchurch with the 1V05 13.25 Crewe to Cardiff Central. The station, opened in 1858, was once the junction for the Cambrian line to Oswestry and Ellesmere and the LNWR line to Waverton. Both lines were closed by 1965. 22 October 1983.

Opposite below: **92. Passing the** signal box and the old goods shed, class 33/0 33017 heads north from Whitchurch with the 1M70 07.40 Cardiff Central to Crewe. Whitchurch signal box, previously named Whitchurch Goods Yard signal box, was a LNWR type 4 design, opened in 1897. It was fitted with a 55 lever frame. The box closed in 2011 and was demolished the following year. 22 October 1983.

SHREWSBURY TO CREWE • 73

93. Six years after the previous photo, the semaphore signals and the goods shed at Whitchurch have gone. Here, viewed from the same vantage point, class 37/4 37422 heads north from the station with the 1M11 07.05 Cardiff Central to Liverpool Lime Street. 13 May 1989.

Opposite above: **94. Class 47/4** 47571 heads the 15.35 Cardiff Central to Crewe through Whitchurch. 5 April 1988.

Opposite below: **95. Class 33/0** 'Crompton' 33017 approaches Whitchurch with the 1V05 13.25 Crewe to Cardiff Central. 22 October 1983.

SHREWSBURY TO CREWE • 75

96. Class 47/4 47621 *Royal County of Berkshire* passes Wrenbury with the 09.15 Liverpool Lime Street to Cardiff Central. The station, nine miles from Crewe, was opened in 1858 by the Crewe and Shrewsbury Railway. 13 May 1989.

Opposite above: **97. Class 37/4** 37429 *Eisteddfod Genedlaethol* heads south through Wrenbury with the 17.19 Crewe to Cardiff Central. 10 September 1987.

Opposite below: **98. Class 37/4** 37430 *Cwmbran* passes Wrenbury with the 1V09 17.19 Crewe to Cardiff Central. Wrenbury signal box, opened in 1882, was a LNWR type 4 design fitted with a 20 lever frame. It closed in 2013 and was demolished in August 2015. 5 April 1988.

SHREWSBURY TO CREWE • 77

99. The old single storey station building is clearly shown in this photograph of Wrenbury, as class 37/4 37431 *Sir Powys/County of Powys* approaches the level crossing as it heads north. 5 April 1988.

Opposite above: **100. Class 108 DMU** set 946, forming the 11.55 Crewe to Swansea service, passes Nantwich Station signal box as it departs from Nantwich. The signal box dates from the 1940s and contains a 30 lever frame. It was closed in 2013 and moved to the Railway Exchange Training Academy at Crewe in 2016. 5 April 1988.

Opposite below: **101. Nantwich railway** station, opened in 1858, was the junction for the GWR line to Market Drayton until 1963. Here, a two-car Metro-Cammell class 101 DMU, forming a Shrewsbury to Crewe service, heads away from the camera as it departs from the station. 22 October 1983.

SHREWSBURY TO CREWE • 79

102. Crewe railway station, located on the electrified West Coast Main Line, was opened in 1837. It has twelve platforms and is 158 miles from London Euston and 243 miles from Glasgow Central. It is the junction for the lines to Manchester, Liverpool, Holyhead, Stoke-on-Trent and Shrewsbury. Here, class 87 Bo-Bo 25 kV AC electric 87002 *Royal Sovereign* heads south from the station with an unidentified working. This class 87 is now owned by Locomotive Services Limited and is used on special trains. 29 December 1982.

Opposite above: **103. Class 40** 40168 waits for departure time from platform 5 at Crewe with the 1K38 17.37 Llandudno to Stoke-on-Trent. The locomotive was withdrawn from service two years later. 13 September 1982.

Opposite below: **104. British Rail** class 304 electric multiple unit 304 036, forming the 22.40 to Liverpool Lime Street, waits to depart from platform 10 at Crewe. 15 November 1987. *(Steve Turner Photo)*

SHREWSBURY TO CREWE • 81

105. Class 50 50024 *Vanguard* stands at platform 8 at Crewe station after arriving with the 20.00 from Cardiff Central. 15 November 1987. *(Steve Turner Photo)*

SHREWSBURY TO WELLINGTON

106. Substituting for the usual class 47/4, class 31/4 diesel-electrics 31405 and 31412 head a Shrewsbury to London Euston service away from the station and under the large signal gantry just west of Abbey Foregate signal box. 30 January 1988.

107. A class 116/101 hybrid three-car DMU, forming a service from Wolverhampton, approaches Abbey Foregate signal box as it heads for Shrewsbury station. The signal box, built to a GWR design, opened in 1914. 7 September 1985.

Opposite above: **108. Viewed from** the Monkmoor Road bridge, class 150 Sprinter 150 107 shunts near Abbey Foregate signal box. This is the site of the former Abbey Foregate station. Opened by the Shrewsbury and Birmingham Railway in 1849, it closed in 1912. There were also goods facilities on both sides of the line. 28 March 1987.

Opposite below: **109. Looking towards** Wolverhampton from the Monkmoor Road bridge, class 47/4 47517 *Andrew Carnegie* approaches Abbey Foregate with the 13.30 London Euston to Shrewsbury. 14 September 1991.

SHREWSBURY TO WELLINGTON • 85

110. Class 37/0 37274, in Railfreight Coal Sector livery, passes the site of Upton Magna station with four loaded coal wagons bound for Shrewsbury. Upton Magna station opened in 1849 and was closed in 1964. 29 July 1989.

Opposite above: **111. With the** A5 Dual Carriageway on the left, class 150 Sprinter 150 108 and a second Sprinter head east at Upton Magna. The working is the 13.25 Aberystwyth to Birmingham New Street. 7 September 1991.

Opposite below: **112. Class 47/4** 47621 *Royal County of Berkshire* passes Walcot with the 1A44 10.13 Aberystwyth to London Euston. Walcot station, closed in 1964, was located near the bridge in the background. 29 July 1989.

SHREWSBURY TO WELLINGTON • 87

113. Class 47/4 47432 passes Walcot with the 11.32 Shrewsbury to London Euston. Note the DVT behind the locomotive. 7 September 1991.

Opposite above: **114. Class 37/4** 37428 *David Lloyd George* passes Walcot with the 09.03 London Euston to Pwllheli, 'The Snowdonian'. The chimneys of Allscott sugar beet factory can just be seen in the background. 8 September 1990.

Opposite below: **115. Class 31/1** diesel-electrics 31146 *Brush Veteran* and 31147 *Floreat Salopia* head the 1J02 09.57 Birmingham New Street to Pwllheli past Walcot. The Allscott sugar beet factory, in the background, closed in 2006 and was demolished in 2008. 26 June 1993.

SHREWSBURY TO WELLINGTON • 89

116. A class 116/101 three-car DMU, forming a Shrewsbury to Wolverhampton service, passes Allscott Sugar Works signal box. The LNWR type 5 signal box was located opposite Allscott sugar beet refinery. Opened in 1928, it was fitted with a 72 lever frame. The signal box was closed and replaced by a ground frame in 1985. 24 March 1984.

Opposite above: **117. Class 47/4** 47436 passes the goods yard, as it accelerates away from the Wellington station stop, with a London Euston to Shrewsbury service. 2 January 1987.

Opposite below: **118. Class 47/4** 47457 *Ben Line* approaches Wellington with the 1A81 15.06 Aberystwyth to London Euston. 29 July 1989.

SHREWSBURY TO WELLINGTON • 91

119. Class 45 45069 runs through the down middle road at Wellington as it heads the 6V34 12.27 Albion Gulf O.D. to Waterston Sidings oil tanks towards Shrewsbury. Wellington station, on the Wolverhampton to Shrewsbury line, was opened in 1849. Once a busy junction station, it had six operational platforms. 4 January 1986.

Opposite above: 120. Class 37/4 37429 *Eisteddfod Genedlaethol* accelerates away from a signal check as it heads the 1A52 09.32 Pwllheli to London Euston, 'The Snowdonian', through the up middle road at Wellington. 18 August 1990.

Opposite below: 121. Class 31/4 31414 passes Wellington No. 2 signal box and approaches Wellington station as it heads west with a permanent way train loaded with track panels. 27 January 1990.

SHREWSBURY TO WELLINGTON • 93

122. With a DVT behind the locomotive, class 47/4 47431 departs from Wellington with the 1A63 15.31 Shrewsbury to London Euston. 29 July 1989.

Opposite: **123. In July** 1991, the Branch Line Society ran 'The Donnington Farewell' railtour from Manchester Piccadilly to Donnington, Bilston, Rugeley and Brereton Sidings. Here, class 37/0 37070 leads the special train away from Wellington towards Stafford Junction and the Donnington branch. Class 37/4 37430 *Cwmbran* is on the back of the train. 6 July 1991.

SHREWSBURY TO WELLINGTON • **95**

WELLINGTON TO DONNINGTON

Left: **124. A class 116/115** hybrid three-car DMU, forming a Wolverhampton to Shrewsbury service, passes Stafford Junction, near Wellington. At this time, the former Stafford line served MoD Donnington. 2 January 1987.

Opposite above: **125. The Stafford** to Shrewsbury Railway opened in 1849, with the section from Stafford to Donnington closing in the 1960s. Here, class 37/0 37070 leads the Branch Line Society's 'The Donnington Farewell' railtour away from Stafford Junction and along the remaining section of the Stafford line to Donnington. Class 37/4 37430 *Cwmbran* is on the rear of the train. 6 July 1991.

WELLINGTON TO DONNINGTON • 97

Below: **126. Class 37/4** 37430 *Cwmbran*, in InterCity livery, trails at the rear of the Branch Line Society's 'The Donnington Farewell' railtour, as the special train heads down the branch to Donnington from Stafford Junction. 6 July 1991.

127. Class 37/0 37070 stands at the closed Trench Crossing railway station with the Branch Line Society's 'The Donnington Farewell' railtour, while the crossing gates are opened for the train to proceed to MoD Donnington. Class 37/4 37430 *Cwmbran* is on the back of the train. The station opened in 1849 and was closed in 1964. 6 July 1991.

WELLINGTON TO DONNINGTON • 99

128. Class 31/4 31454, with the 6T71 MoD Donnington to Shrewsbury Coton Hill freight, waits outside the closed Trench Crossing railway station as the gates are opened. The trip freight's short train is made up of loaded Warwell wagons on this occasion. The MoD facility is beyond the gates. 25 July 1988. *(Paul Dorney Photo)*

WELLINGTON TO MADELEY JUNCTION

129. Class 37/4 37429 *Eisteddfod Genedlaethol* pauses at Telford Central station with the 1A52 09.32 Pwllheli to London Euston, 'The Snowdonian'. Telford Central station was opened in 1986, between Wellington and Oakengates, to serve the new town of Telford. 8 September 1990.

130. Class 47/4 47621 *Royal County of Berkshire* heads the 14.04 Shrewsbury to London Euston through Oakengates station. In the background, class 37/4 37427 *Bont Y Bermo* shunts cement tanks from Penyfford Cement Sidings at the Tunnel Cement Terminal. 13 October 1989. *(Paul Dorney Photo)*

MADELEY JUNCTION TO IRONBRIDGE

131. Class 58 58035 heads a train of empty HAA coal hopper wagons, from Ironbridge Power Station, onto the Shrewsbury to Wolverhampton line at Madeley Junction, between Telford Central and Shifnal. Madeley Junction signal box, a British Railways (London Midland Region) type 15 design, opened in 1969 and was closed in November 2012. 23 July 1987.

Opposite above: **132. There were** two Ironbridge power stations, located next to the River Severn at Buildwas. The first was commissioned in 1932 and decommissioned in 1969. The second, larger, power station operated from 1981 until 2015. Here, class 60 60093 heads an empty coal train from the power station, bound for Chatterley Valley, between Lightmoor Junction and Madeley Junction. 16 February 1993. *(Paul Dorney Photo)*

MADELEY JUNCTION TO IRONBRIDGE • **103**

Below: **133. Class 20** diesel-electrics 20106 and 20113 pause at Lightmoor Junction, with an empty coal train from Ironbridge Power Station, while the token for the single line to Madeley Junction is collected. The British Railways (Western Region) signal box closed in 2006, when the line to Ironbridge Power Station was singled. 21 August 1990. *(Paul Dorney Photo)*

134. From Lightmoor Junction to Ironbridge Power Station, the line is double track. Here, class 20 diesel-electrics 20175 and 20182 cross Coalbrookdale Viaduct with a loaded coal train to Ironbridge Power Station. 26 January 1990. *(Paul Dorney Photo)*

Opposite above: **135. Class 56** 56022 passes Coalbrookdale with a loaded coal train to Ironbridge Power Station. Coalbrookdale Station was opened in 1864 by the Wellington and Severn Junction Railway. It closed in 1962. 12 June 1991. *(Paul Dorney Photo)*

Opposite below: **136. Class 58** 58016 crosses the Albert Edward Bridge over the River Severn at Coalbrookdale, as it approaches Ironbridge Power Station with a loaded coal train. The bridge, opened in 1864, was named after the Prince of Wales. 13 March 1993.

MADELEY JUNCTION TO IRONBRIDGE • **105**

137. Class 20 diesel-electrics 20121 and 20141 prepare to run round their coal train from Silverdale Colliery, prior to entering Ironbridge Power Station to discharge their coal. 2 February 1990. *(Paul Dorney Photo)*

MADELEY JUNCTION TO WOLVERHAMPTON

138. **Class 20** diesel-electric locomotives 20045 and 20169 head an empty coal train from Ironbridge Power Station onto the Shrewsbury to Wolverhampton line at Madeley Junction. 15 September 1990.

139. With the Trinity Methodist Church in the background, Class 47/4 47456 heads the diverted 10.10 Manchester Piccadilly to Birmingham New Street through Shifnal. Shifnal station opened in 1849. 11 September 1988. *(David Rostance Photo)*

Opposite above: **140. An unidentified** Class 47 approaches Cosford with the 1A49 14.32 Shrewsbury to London Euston. 10 August 1991.

Opposite below: **141. On a** frosty morning, class 47/0 47201 heads west through Cosford with empty oil tanks from Albion Gulf O.D. to Waterston Sidings. Cosford station is in the background. 4 January 1986.

MADELEY JUNCTION TO WOLVERHAMPTON • 109

142. **A class 115/119** hybrid three-car DMU, forming a Shrewsbury to Wolverhampton service, passes Cosford signal box as it approaches the station. The GWR signal box, fitted with a 39 lever frame, dates from 1939. The box closed when control passed to Madeley Junction in 2006. 31 December 1986.

Opposite above: 143. **A class 119/115** hybrid three-car DMU, forming a Shrewsbury to Wolverhampton service, pauses at Cosford station. The station, known as Cosford Aerodrome halt until 1940, serves RAF Cosford and the Royal Air Force Museum, as well as Cosford village. The wooden station buildings and platforms, dating from 1937, were replaced in 2012. 31 December 1986.

Opposite below: 144. **Class 25/3** diesel-electrics 25270 and 25259 head the 10.10 Aberystwyth to London Euston past Albrighton. Albrighton station was opened by the Shrewsbury and Birmingham Railway in 1849. The final year of the class 25 diesel-electrics on the Cambrian summer Saturday trains was 1984. Not only were they replaced by class 37s in 1985, but the system changed whereby two locomotive changes were introduced, the electric being replaced by a class 47 at Wolverhampton and the class 47 by a class 37 at Shrewsbury. 23 September 1978. *(David Rostance Photo)*

MADELEY JUNCTION TO WOLVERHAMPTON • 111

145. A class 116/101 hybrid three-car DMU, forming a Shrewsbury to Wolverhampton service, passes Codsall signal box as it heads away from the Codsall station stop. The GWR signal box, opened in 1929 and fitted with a 25 lever frame, closed when control passed to Madeley Junction following a resignalling scheme in 2006. 4 January 1986.

Opposite above: **146. With the** West Highland Terrier emblem of Eastfield TMD on its bodyside, class 47/4 47595 *Confederation of British Industry* passes Codsall station with the 1A31 09.35 Shrewsbury to London Euston. 25 January 1986.

Opposite below: **147. Class 47/4** 47602 *Glorious Devon* heads west through Codsall station with the 1J20 07.30 London Euston to Aberystwyth. The train will have been hauled by an electric locomotive from Euston to Wolverhampton and class 37/0 37210 will take over the train at Shrewsbury for the journey to Aberystwyth. 31 August 1985.

MADELEY JUNCTION TO WOLVERHAMPTON • 113

148. Class 58 58005 heads an empty coal train, from Ironbridge Power Station, east through Codsall station. The station is located four and a half miles west of Wolverhampton on the former GWR line to Shrewsbury. The GWR footbridge dates from 1883. The station house, on the left, was converted into a public house, 'The Station', in 1999. 27 October 1990.

Opposite above: **149. Class 87** 25 kV AC electric locomotive 87004 *Britannia* leads the stock of a London Euston to Wolverhampton train across the viaduct over the Birmingham Main Line Canal at Oxley, near Wolverhampton, towards Oxley carriage sidings. 4 March 1989.

Opposite below: **150. Class 37/0** 37154, in Transrail livery, stands at Wolverhampton after arriving with the First North Western 11.16 Bangor to Birmingham New Street service. The station, located on the Birmingham Loop of the West Coast Main Line, was originally named Wolverhampton Queen Street and was opened in 1852 by the Birmingham, Wolverhampton and Stour Valley Railway, a subsidiary of the LNWR. The station was renamed Wolverhampton High Level in 1885, following the opening of the GWR Wolverhampton Low Level station. It was rebuilt between 1964 and 1967. 31 July 1999. *(David Rostance Photo)*

MADELEY JUNCTION TO WOLVERHAMPTON • 115

151. Class 47/4 47814 *Totnes Castle* arrives at Wolverhampton with the 1S76 09.18 Brighton to Edinburgh Virgin Cross Country service. This locomotive was one of the class 47/4s fitted with extra fuel tanks. Wolverhampton station has four through and two bay platforms and is the junction of the lines to Stafford, Birmingham, and Shrewsbury. 31 July 1999. *(David Rostance Photo)*

MADELEY JUNCTION TO WOLVERHAMPTON • 117

152. On a rainy day, Class 37/4 37414 *Cathays C&W Works 1846-1993* stands at Wolverhampton with the 1D68 09.46 Birmingham International to Holyhead. 1 October 1994. *(David Rostance Photo)*

SHREWSBURY TO ABBEY

153. Class 08 diesel-electric shunter 08585 reverses its oil-tank train from Coton Hill Yard, at Sutton Bridge Junction, to gain access to the line to Shrewsbury Abbey. 10 September 1987.

154. With the abbey in the background, Class 08 diesel-electric shunter 08585 shunts its train from Coton Hill Yard into the Esso oil terminal at Shrewsbury Abbey. Traffic to Shrewsbury Abbey ended in July 1988. Shrewsbury Abbey railway station, opened in 1866 by the Potteries, Shrewsbury and North Wales Railway, closed in 1880. In 1911, it was reopened and became the terminus of the Shropshire and Montgomeryshire Railway at Shrewsbury The station had a goods yard, later the site of the oil terminal, and a wagon works. The crane was made in the Abbey Works. 10 September 1987.

SHREWSBURY TO WELSHPOOL

Above: **155. The crew** of class 37/0 37233 prepare for token duties at Sutton Bridge Junction, Shrewsbury. The second locomotive is 37251 and the working is the 1J20 07.30 London Euston to Pwllheli. 2 August 1986.

Opposite above: **156. Class 25** 25262 stands at Sutton Bridge Junction with a permanent way train. The lines to Hereford and Aberystwyth divide at the junction. It was also the junction for the Severn Valley Railway line to Hartlebury, near Droitwich Spa, closed in 1963. 31 August 1985.

Opposite below: **157. Class 08** diesel-electric shunter 08737 shunts a short train of track panels into Coleham Civil Engineer's Depot at Sutton Bridge Junction. 2 August 1986.

SHREWSBURY TO WELSHPOOL • **121**

158. Sutton Bridge Junction signal box is located next to Sutton Lane bridge in Shrewsbury. The box, opened in 1913 replacing an earlier box, is a GWR type 7d design fitted with a 61 lever frame. The Severn Valley Railway line ran behind the box. 18 August 1990.

Opposite above: **159. Class 47/0** 47200 approaches Sutton Bridge Junction with a train of welded rail from Hookagate permanent way depot, located on the line to Welshpool. The lines on the left lead to Hereford. 31 August 1985.

Opposite below: **160. Class 37/4** 37431 *Sir Powys/County of Powys* approaches the A5191 Belle Vue Road bridge at Meole Brace, Shrewsbury, with the 1A31 07.13 Aberystwyth to London Euston. The locomotive's headboard reads 'Cambrian Railways 125 Years 1864-1989'. 29 July 1989.

SHREWSBURY TO WELSHPOOL • 123

124 • RAILS FROM SHREWSBURY

161. With the houses along Drawwell Street on the left, class 31/1 diesel-electrics 31146 and 31166, in Civil Engineer's grey and yellow livery, head the 2J23 09.25 Birmingham New Street to Pwllheli away from Shrewsbury, past Meole Brace. 22 August 1992.

Opposite above: **162. Class 37/0** 37208 heads the 1A50 11.10 Aberystwyth to London Euston past Hookagate, near Shrewsbury. Note the wagons at the permanent way depot in the distance. Hookagate and Redhill station opened in 1866 and closed in 1933. 7 September 1985.

Opposite below: **163. Class 37/0** 37176 enters the loop as it arrives at Westbury with the 1J24 09.35 London Euston to Aberystwyth. 31 August 1985.

SHREWSBURY TO WELSHPOOL • 125

126 • RAILS FROM SHREWSBURY

164. The signalman waits with the token, as class 37/4 37426 *Y Lein Fach/Vale of Rheidol* arrives at Westbury with the 1A50 11.10 Aberystwyth to London Euston. The passing loop and LNWR/GWR Joint type 1 signal box remained until 1988, when control passed to the signalling centre at Machynlleth. 2 August 1986.

Opposite above: **165. A class 120/101** hybrid three-car DMU, forming a Shrewsbury to Aberystwyth service, pauses in the loop at Westbury while tokens are exchanged, before continuing its journey west. Westbury station, opened in 1861 by the Shrewsbury and Welshpool Railway, was closed in 1960. The station building is now a private residence. 31 August 1985.

Opposite below: **166. Class 37/4** 37431 departs from Welshpool with the up 'Cambrian Coast Express', the 07.22 Aberystwyth to London Euston. Note the steam era-style 'Cambrian Coast Express' headboard. A 'Cambrian Coast Express' headboard was carried by the named express from London Paddington to Aberystwyth and Pwllheli in the 1950s and early 1960s. 26 July 1986.

SHREWSBURY TO WELSHPOOL • 127

167. Class 37/0 37194 passes Welshpool signal box as it approaches the station with the 1J24 09.35 London Euston to Aberystwyth. The signal box is a LNWR type 4 design, opened in 1887, replacing an earlier box. Originally named Welshpool North signal box, it was renamed Welshpool around 1931 after Welshpool South signal box was closed. The signal box closed in 1988. 27 July 1985.

Opposite above: **168. On Spring** Bank Holiday Monday 1987, 37427 *Bont Y Bermo*, carrying a 'Cambrian Coast Express' headboard, arrives at Welshpool with the 15.40 London Euston to Aberystwyth. 25 May 1987.

Opposite below: **169. Class 37/0** diesel-electrics 37163 and 37176 wait to depart from Welshpool with the 1J20 07.30 London Euston to Aberystwyth. The station was built by the Oswestry and Newtown Railway, opening in 1860. In 1992, the railway at Welshpool was realigned to make room for the A483 Welshpool bypass and the old station building, now privately-owned, is located on the other side of the road. The new station is an island platform. The former Cambrian Railways narrow gauge line to Llanfair Caereinion, closed by British Railways in 1956 and now in private ownership, also started at Welshpool. 27 July 1985.

SHREWSBURY TO WELSHPOOL • **129**

SHREWSBURY TO CRAVEN ARMS

Above: **170. Class 47/4** 47450 departs from platform 4 at Shrewsbury with the 11.35 Crewe to Cardiff Central service. Class 37/4 37429 *Eisteddfod Genedlaethol* is stabled next to the old platform 2 and, in the distance, a class 150 Sprinter heads north from platform 3. Laura's Tower, a part of Shrewsbury Castle, is in the background. 19 December 1987.

Opposite above: **171. Class 37/7** 37712 *The Cardiff Rod Mill* passes Sutton Bridge Junction, Shrewsbury, with the 6V75 Mossend to Cardiff Tidal Sidings loaded steel coil train. 18 August 1990.

Opposite below: **172. Class 37/4** 37431 and class 37/0 37180 *County of Dyfed/Sir Dyfed* head south, past Sutton Bridge Junction, with the 3V20 15.10 Manchester to Bristol Temple Meads parcels. 27 September 1986.

SHREWSBURY TO CRAVEN ARMS • 131

132 • RAILS FROM SHREWSBURY

173. Class 37/7 locomotives 37897 and 37802 pass Sutton Bridge Junction, Shrewsbury, with the 1Z16 11.00 Hereford to Crewe special train. The line from Welshpool is above the locomotives. The train was one of a number run by Regional Railways in association with open days at Hereford and Coton Hill Yard, Shrewsbury. The leading locomotive carries two headboards which read 'The Wye Knot' and 'The Jim Molloy Ding Dong Special'. 30 May 1993.

Opposite above: **174. An unidentified** class 40 heads south from Shrewsbury, near Bayston Hill, with a short train of loaded forty ton ballast hoppers. The railway from Shrewsbury to Hereford was opened as a standard gauge line in 1853 by the Shrewsbury and Hereford Railway Company. 2 October 1976.

Opposite below: **175. Class 33/0** 'Cromptons' 33051 *Shakespeare Cliff* and 33030 head the returning Pathfinder Tours' 'The Crompton Culminator' railtour, from Salisbury to Holyhead, back to Bristol Temple Meads. The special train is pictured approaching Bayston Hill. 6 September 1997.

SHREWSBURY TO CRAVEN ARMS • 133

176. Metro-Cammell class 101 two-car DMU set C800, forming a Shrewsbury to Swansea service, passes Bayston Hill. Bayston Hill Quarry is in the background. 20 December 1986.

Opposite above: **177. Class 108 DMU** set S950, forming the 15.15 Crewe to Swansea, rounds a long curve as it heads south towards Dorrington. 13 May 1989.

Opposite below: **178. Class 37/0** diesel-electrics 37177 and 37224 are pictured north of Dorrington, heading south with a loaded steel coil train. 20 December 1986.

SHREWSBURY TO CRAVEN ARMS • **135**

179. Class 47/4 47421 heads north past Dorrington with the 1M17 13.23 Cardiff Central to Liverpool Lime Street. The locomotive was named *The Brontes of Haworth* until the end of September of the previous year and the area where the nameplate was carried can be seen on the bodyside of the locomotive. 13 May 1989.

Opposite above: **180. Class 37/4** diesel-electrics 37427 *Bont Y Bermo* and 37426 *Y Lein Fach/ Vale of Rheidol* pass the site of Dorrington station with the 3V20 15.10 Manchester to Bristol Temple Meads parcels. Dorrington station opened in 1852 and was closed in 1958. The signal box is a LNWR/GWR Joint type 1 design opened circa 1872. 2 August 1986.

Opposite below: **181. Metro-Cammell class 101** two-car DMU set C801, forming a Shrewsbury to Swansea service via the Central Wales line, passes All Stretton, north of Church Stretton on the Welsh Marches line. 13 December 1986.

SHREWSBURY TO CRAVEN ARMS • 137

182. Class 37/9 37901 *Mirrlees Pioneer* approaches Church Stretton with a southbound steel train. 30 January 1988.

Opposite above: **183. With the** goods loop in the foreground, class 47/0 47100 approaches Church Stretton as it heads south with a loaded steel train. 29 November 1986.

Opposite below: **184. Class 33/0** 33022 passes Church Stretton signal box with the 1V09 14.08 Holyhead to Cardiff Central. The box, a LNWR/GWR Joint type 1 box dating from around 1872, closed in 2003. This signal box design was used in various locations on the lines from Shrewsbury. The goods loop was removed around 1990. 16 August 1986.

SHREWSBURY TO CRAVEN ARMS • **139**

185. Class 33/0 'Crompton' 33016 arrives at Church Stretton with a Crewe to Cardiff Central service. The present-day station at Church Stretton was opened in 1914 to the south of the original station, which dated from 1852. 31 August 1983.

Opposite above: **186. A two-car** Metro-Cammell class 101 DMU, forming a Shrewsbury to Swansea service, heads south near Church Stretton. 6 December 1986.

Opposite below: **187. Class 37/9** 37904 heads a southbound steel train past Little Stretton, south of Church Stretton. 9 April 1988.

SHREWSBURY TO CRAVEN ARMS • 141

188. Class 117 DMU set T308, forming the 10.03 Swansea to Crewe, passes Little Stretton as it heads north towards the Church Stretton station stop. 9 April 1988.

Opposite above: **189. Class 47/4** 47561 approaches Marshbrook level crossing as it heads south with the 13.45 Manchester Piccadilly to Cardiff Central. 28 March 1987.

Opposite below: **190. Metro-Cammell class 101 DMU** set C800, forming a Shrewsbury to Swansea service, approaches Marshbrook level crossing. Marshbrook signal box, built to a LNWR/GWR Joint type 1 design, dates from around 1872. It is a Grade II listed building. Although the hamlet is usually referred to as Marshbrook, the plate on the box says Marsh Brook. Marshbrook station opened in 1852 and closed in 1958. 14 February 1987.

SHREWSBURY TO CRAVEN ARMS • **143**

191. Class 47/3 47354 rounds the curve at Wistanstow, north of Craven Arms, with the partially loaded 4V68 Holyhead to Pengam FLT container train. The locomotive is painted in Railfreight Distribution livery. 8 September 1990.

Opposite above: **192. The class 127 DMUs,** with hydraulic transmission, were built at Derby in 1959. In 1985, eleven two-car diesel parcel units (DPUs) were produced using the power cars from class 127 four-car DMUs. Here, DPU set 912, made up of 55982 and 55972, leads a second unit and a van round one of the curves north of Craven Arms. Both DPUs are fitted with roller shutter doors. The working is the Saturdays Only 15.10 Manchester to Cardiff parcels, with one set continuing to Bristol. All the DPUs were withdrawn two days later. 13 May 1989.

Opposite below: **193. Former Glasgow** Eastfield class 37/4 37422 is pictured near Cheney Longville, heading the 1M48 15.55 Cardiff Central to Liverpool Lime Street away from Craven Arms. 13 May 1989.

SHREWSBURY TO CRAVEN ARMS • **145**

194. Class 37/9 37906 heads an empty steel train, towards Craven Arms, at Long Lane level crossing, north of the station. In 2000, the GWR signal box was rebuilt and enlarged by building a clad steel-framed structure around it before removing the original wooden structure inside. 9 April 1988.

Opposite above: **195. Craven Arms** station, located twenty miles south of Shrewsbury, was named Craven Arms and Stokesay until 1974. It is the junction of the lines to Shrewsbury, Hereford and the Central Wales line to Swansea. Until 1935, Craven Arms was also the eastern terminus of the Bishops Castle Railway. Here, class 33/0 33035 arrives at the station with the 1V05 13.45 Manchester Piccadilly to Cardiff Central. 19 April 1986.

Opposite below: **196. As a** DMU heads north from the station, 37427 *Bont Y Bermo* approaches Craven Arms with the 1V08 09.15 Liverpool Lime Street to Cardiff Central. On the left are the carriage sheds, now demolished. The former goods shed is on the right. 6 August 1988.

SHREWSBURY TO CRAVEN ARMS • 147

CRAVEN ARMS TO KNIGHTON

197. Metro-Cammell class 101 DMU set C800 takes the line to Knighton and Swansea, as it heads away from the camera at Craven Arms. The working is a Shrewsbury to Swansea service, via the Central Wales line. 9 April 1986.

Opposite above: **198. Class 153 Super** Sprinter 153 312, forming the 2V06 16.02 Shrewsbury to Swansea service, pauses at Hopton Heath on the Central Wales line. The class 153 railcars were converted from two-car class 155 units. 17 July 1994. *(Steve Turner Photo)*

Opposite below: **199. Class 37/4** diesel-electrics 37401 *Mary Queen of Scots* and 37426 pass Hopton Heath with the diverted 6M24 Margam to Dee Marsh loaded steel train. The station was opened by the Knighton Railway in 1861. The station building is now a private residence. 28 May 2000.

CRAVEN ARMS TO KNIGHTON • **149**

200. Class 153 Super Sprinter 153 355, forming the 2V04 13.13 Crewe to Cardiff Central, pauses at Bucknell. The station, located between Hopton Heath and Knighton, was opened in 1861. The station building, a Grade II listed building, is now a private residence and holiday cottage. 28 May 2000. *(Steve Turner Photo)*

Opposite above: **201. After travelling** over the Central Wales line, class 37/4 37408 *Loch Rannoch* is pictured at Stowe, east of Knighton, as it heads the Regency Rail Cruise 'The Welsh Rambler' from York and Leeds towards Bucknell and Craven Arms. 8 November 1997.

Opposite below: **202. Passengers wait** at Knighton as Metro-Cammell class 101 DMU set C803, forming the 10.50 Shrewsbury to Swansea service, approaches the station. The station, built in 1865, serves the town of Knighton in Powys, Wales, although the station itself is actually just in England. 19 April 1986.

CRAVEN ARMS TO KNIGHTON • **151**

152 • RAILS FROM SHREWSBURY

203. Class 153 Super Sprinter 153 303, forming the 2M37 12.40 Swansea to Crewe, arrives at Knighton. The passing loop, removed in 1964, was reinstated in 1990, after the modernisation of the signalling along the line in 1986. 17 September 1995. *(Steve Turner Photo)*

CRAVEN ARMS TO KNIGHTON • **153**

204. Looking west from Knighton, 66152 approaches the station with the diverted 6M82 08.40 Margam TC to Hardendale Quarry limestone empties. From Knighton, the line continues through Llandrindod Wells and past Sugar Loaf summit, 820ft above sea level, reaching Swansea via Pantyffynnon. 28 May 2000. *(Steve Turner Photo)*

CRAVEN ARMS TO HEREFORD

Above: **205. After running** round its train at Craven Arms, class 37/0 37178 passes Stokesay Castle as it heads south with the 8L61 13.00 Bromfield to Newport Alexandra Dock Junction empty ballast train. 25 June 1995. *(Steve Turner Photo)*

Opposite above: **206. Freightliner class 70** 70010 heads north as it approaches Onibury level crossing with a train of imported coal from Portbury. The small BR (Western Region) signal box, opened in the late 1970s replacing an earlier box, stands opposite the old station building, now a private residence. The station at Onibury opened in 1852 and closed in 1958. 24 November 2012. *(Paul Dorney Photo)*

Opposite below: **207. Class 37/4** 37411 heads the 8Z11 13.30 Church Stretton to Newport Alexandra Dock Junction permanent way train across the bridge over the River Onny and towards Onibury level crossing. 9 April 1995. *(Steve Turner Photo)*

CRAVEN ARMS TO HEREFORD • **155**

208. After passing Onibury, class 37/7 37711 *Tremorfa Steelworks* heads a southbound steel train towards Bromfield. Loaded four-wheel scrap wagons are behind the covered steel carrier at the front of the train. 13 May 1989.

Opposite above: **209. Class 33/0** 33032 heads north, past Bromfield level crossing, with the 1M68 06.12 Cardiff Central to Crewe. The signal box was built to a LNWR/GWR Joint type 1 design, and dates from circa 1872. Bromfield station, opened in 1852 by the Shrewsbury and Hereford Railway, was closed in 1958. 6 September 1986.

Opposite below: **210. Class 37/4** 37428 *David Lloyd George* waits to depart from Ludlow with the 1V09 10.00 Manchester Piccadilly to Cardiff Central. Opened in 1852 by the Shrewsbury and Hereford Railway, the station buildings were demolished in the late 1960s and replaced by small shelters on each platform. The goods yard closed in 1968 but the goods shed still remains and can be seen in the background. 25 February 1989.

CRAVEN ARMS TO HEREFORD • 157

211. Class 47/4 47526 *Northumbria* exits the short Ludlow Tunnel under Gravel Hill, just to the south of the station, with the 1V03 05.15 Holyhead to Cardiff Central. 9 April 1988.

Opposite above: **212. With snow** on the ground, class 156 Super Sprinter 156 464, forming the 09.14 Cardiff Central to Liverpool Lime Street, is pictured near Ludlow. St Laurence's church is in the background. 25 February 1989.

Opposite below: **213. Class 33/0** 'Cromptons' 33051 *Shakespeare Cliff* and 33030 pass Woofferton, as they head back to Bristol Temple Meads with 'The Crompton Culminator' railtour. Pathfinder Tours ran the special train from Salisbury to Holyhead, with class 47/7 47738 providing the traction between Salisbury and Bristol Temple Meads. Woofferton station was opened in 1853 on the Shrewsbury and Hereford Railway and later became the junction station for the line to Tenbury and Bewdley. It was closed in 1961. The former station building and goods shed are on the right. 6 September 1997.

CRAVEN ARMS TO HEREFORD • 159

214. Class 33/0 33030 passes the signal box as it heads north at Woofferton with the 1M70 07.50 Swansea to Manchester Piccadilly. Woofferton Junction signal box is a LNWR/GWR Joint type 1 design, opened in 1875. The box was later extended to accommodate a larger frame. 26 April 1986.

Opposite above: **215. Class 47/7** 47792 *Saint Cuthbert*, in Rail Express Systems livery, passes Woofferton with a special train from Liverpool Lime Street to Cardiff Central. The train ran in connection with the Football League Cup Final between Liverpool and Birmingham City at the Millenium Stadium, Cardiff. 25 February 2001.

Opposite below: **216. Class 33/0** 33035 heads north at Woofferton with the 1M70 07.50 Swansea to Manchester Piccadilly. 19 April 1986.

CRAVEN ARMS TO HEREFORD • 161

217. Class 37/4 37427 *Bont Y Bermo* stands at Leominster with the 1M84 10.45 Cardiff Central to Crewe. Leominster station, opened in 1853, is located eleven miles north of Hereford. It was the junction station for the Leominster and Kington Railway, closed in 1955, and the Worcester, Bromyard and Leominster Railway, closed to Bromyard in 1952. 31 August 1987.

Opposite above: 218. Class 60 60072 passes the LNWR/GWR Joint type 1 signal box as it approaches Leominster station with a Llanwern to Dee Marsh steel train. 28 May 2001.

Opposite below: 219. Class 67 diesel-electrics 67023 and 67026 head south through Leominster with the 'South Devon Express', the 1Z89 06.37 Hooton to Plymouth. The train was organised by the Chester Model Railway Club and the Dee and Mersey Group of the Ffestiniog Railway. 21 April 2007.

CRAVEN ARMS TO HEREFORD • **163**

164 • RAILS FROM SHREWSBURY

220. Class 66 diesel-electrics 66062 and 66167 head a loaded Margam to Dee Marsh steel train towards Leominster. 19 August 2000.

Opposite above: **221. Class 37/7** 37887 heads a southbound empty steel train between Leominster and Ford Bridge. 25 February 1989.

Opposite below: **222. Class 37/4** 37422 heads north from Ford Bridge with the 1M17 13.23 Cardiff Central to Liverpool Lime Street. 25 February 1989.

CRAVEN ARMS TO HEREFORD • 165

223. **Class 47/4** 47557 passes the old station building and the LNWR/GWR Joint type 1 signal box at Ford Bridge level crossing, as it heads south with the 13.45 Manchester Piccadilly to Cardiff Central. Ford Bridge station, opened in 1854, was closed in 1954. 2 May 1987.

Opposite above: **224. The two** railway tunnels between Leominster and Hereford, to the south of Hope under Dinmore, are known as the Dinmore Tunnels. The first of the tunnels was built in 1853 and the second in 1891. Here, class 150 Sprinter 150 269, forming the 11.20 Liverpool Lime Street to Pembroke Dock, exits the later of the two tunnels as it heads for Hereford. 13 August 1988.

Opposite below: **225. Class 47/4** 47433 heads south past Moreton-on-Lugg with a southbound loaded steel train. The station, opened in 1853, closed to passengers in 1958, closing completely in 1964. The signal box, a GWR type 12c design fitted with a 44 lever frame, opened in 1943 replacing an earlier box. 26 April 1986.

CRAVEN ARMS TO HEREFORD • 167

168 • RAILS FROM SHREWSBURY

Above: **226. Having passed** Shelwick Junction, where the line from Worcester joins the Shrewsbury to Hereford line, class 33/0 33032 approaches Hereford station with the 1V04 10.00 Crewe to Cardiff Central. On the left is Brecon Curve signal box, a LNWR/GWR Joint type 2 box built by the Railway Signal Company, with the remains of the Brecon line diverging from the main line in front of it. The box has since been demolished. The tall metal structures in the background are at the premises of Painter Brothers Ltd, fabricators of structural steelwork. 5 June 1982.

Opposite above: **227. Class 40** 40106 passes Brecon Curve signal box as it departs from Hereford with the 'Welsh Marches Pullman'. The train ran from London Euston, with GWR 4-6-0s 4930 *Hagley Hall* and 7812 *Erlestoke Manor* heading the train from Shrewsbury to Hereford and 40106 taking the train back to Crewe. The class 40 now belongs to the The Class 40 Preservation Society. The line curving away to the right is the remains of the line to Brecon, which led to Bulmer's Railway Centre at this time. 17 April 1982.

Opposite below: **228. In May** 1991, a railway event was held at Hereford. Locomotives displayed at the Rail Day included 20007, 20032, 26038, 31405, 47575, 90043, D1842, and D7523. Special trains also ran using a variety of motive power, and class 121 single-car DMU T013 55013 provided a shuttle service between Hereford station and Bulmer's Railway Centre. Steam locomotives based at the centre included GWR 4-6-0 *King George V*. Here, the 'Bubble Car' heads away from Barton and Brecon Curve Junction towards the railway centre. The line that carries straight on beyond the bridge previously joined the Hereford to Shrewsbury line at Barr's Court Junction. The line branching away on the left originally ran to the gas works. These lines later served industrial premises, including Painter Brothers and Henry Wiggins. 5 May 1991.

CRAVEN ARMS TO HEREFORD • 169

229. A railway open day was held at Hereford in 1993, at the same time as an open day at Coton Hill Yard, Shrewsbury. Regional Railways ran special trains between the locations, as well as to other destinations. Here, class 60 60093 stands at the front of one of the lines of locomotives on display. Other types present include classes 25, 31, 33, 37, 47, 50, 52, 56 and 73. 30 May 1993.

Opposite above: **230. Class 37/0** 37191, in Civil Engineer's grey and yellow livery, departs from Hereford with the 2M33 13.05 Cardiff Central to Liverpool Lime Street. Opened as Hereford Barr's Court station in 1853, the station was renamed Hereford in 1893. Located on the line from Shrewsbury to Newport and Cardiff, it is the junction station for the line to Worcester. 8 August 1993.

Opposite below: **231. Class 37/0** 37271, Class 37/3 37300 and an unidentified class 47 stand next to Hereford station. The Victorian Gothic station building was designed by R.E. Johnson. 9 April 1983.

CRAVEN ARMS TO HEREFORD • 171

172 • RAILS FROM SHREWSBURY

232. Class 47/4 47571 passes Hereford signal box as it arrives at Hereford with the 1M86 16.35 Cardiff Central to Holyhead. The signal box is a LNWR/GWR Joint type 2 design, built by the Railway Signal Company in 1884. It was known as Ayleston Hill until 1973. 3 April 1988.

Opposite above: **233. Class 37/5** 37693 shunts a ballast train at the south end of Hereford station. 28 June 1987.

Opposite below: **234. Class 47/4** 47503 approaches Hereford station with the 1M86 16.35 Cardiff Central to Holyhead. Standing next to the main line is class 50 50021 *Rodney* with the stock of a train to London Paddington, with class 116 DMU set C394 alongside. Class 108 DMU set B973 and class 116 DMU set T338 stand at the fuelling point. 1 May 1988.

CRAVEN ARMS TO HEREFORD • 173

STEAM-HAULED SPECIAL TRAINS

235. Designed by Sir William Stanier, Princess Royal class 4-6-2 6201 *Princess Elizabeth* was built in 1933 by the London, Midland and Scottish Railway (LMSR) at Crewe Works. Withdrawn in 1962, the locomotive was bought by the Princess Elizabeth Locomotive Society and moved to the Dowty Railway Preservation Society's sidings at Ashchurch, later moving to Bulmer's Railway Centre at Hereford. In 1993, it was moved again, this time to the Midland Railway Centre, Butterley. Here, *Princess Elizabeth* passes Coton Hill Yard, Shrewsbury, as it heads a special train to Chester. Coton Hill North signal box is on the right. 5 May 1978.

236. GWR King class 4-6-0 6000 *King George V* takes water from a road tanker at Baschurch, during a scheduled stop, while working a northbound 'Welsh Marches Pullman' special train. Designed by Charles Collett, the locomotive was built in 1927 at Swindon Works. *King George V* visited North America in August 1927 for the Baltimore & Ohio Centenary, where it was presented with a brass bell and cabside medallions to mark the occasion. Withdrawn in 1962, the locomotive is owned by the National Railway Museum and is now displayed at Swindon. 31 August 1983.

237. Rebuilt Merchant Navy class 4-6-2 35028 *Clan Line* heads south from Wrexham General station with a 'Welsh Marches Express', bound for Shrewsbury. The train ran from London Euston, with *Clan Line* heading the train from Hereford to Chester and back to Shrewsbury. The locomotive was built at Eastleigh Works in 1948 to the design of Oliver Bulleid, rebuilt in 1959, and withdrawn in 1967. 29 September 1984.

Opposite above: **238. In 1986,** the Stephenson Locomotive Society ran a special train from Wolverhampton to Stockport to celebrate W.A. 'Cam' Camwell's eightieth birthday. LNWR Webb Coal Tank 1054 hauled the train from Shrewsbury to Stockport and is pictured here approaching Ruabon. Three hundred of these 0-6-2T locomotives, designed by F. W. Webb, were built between 1881 and 1897. W.A. Camwell, a member of the Stephenson Locomotive Society, was a very active railway enthusiast and photographer. 18 October 1986.

Opposite below: **239. Stanier Pacific** 6201 *Princess Elizabeth* storms past the closed Bersham Colliery, south of Wrexham, with 'The White Rose' railtour, as it heads for Shrewsbury. The train ran from London Kings Cross to York, where 6201 took over the train, returning to London Euston via Shrewsbury. Twelve Princess Royal class express passenger locomotives were built at Crewe between 1933 and 1935. 11 April 1987.

STEAM-HAULED SPECIAL TRAINS • 177

Above: 240. The M&GN Joint Railway Society's 'The Mayflower' railtour approaches the former Condover station building, south of Shrewsbury, behind rebuilt Merchant Navy class 4-6-2 35028 *Clan Line*. *Clan Line* worked the special train from Chester to Hereford. The railtour originated at London Euston, and also used King class 4-6-0 6000 *King George V* between Hereford and Chester. Condover station, opened in 1852, was closed in 1958. 26 April 1975.

Opposite above: 241. Stanier Jubilee class 4-6-0 5690 *Leander*, built at Crewe in 1936, takes water from a road tanker at Dorrington, while heading 'The West Mercian' railtour between Chester and Hereford. The locomotive arrived at Barry Scrapyard in June 1964 and was the eighteenth to leave there for preservation, in May 1972. 28 January 1984.

Opposite below: 242. GWR Castle class 4-6-0 5051 *Drysllwyn Castle*, in Great Western livery, heads 'The Red Dragon' railtour south near All Stretton. The special train, which originated at Swansea, was organised by the Monmouthshire Railway Society to celebrate its twenty-fifth anniversary. Built in 1936, the locomotive was named *Drysllwyn Castle*. In August 1937, it was renamed *Earl Bathurst,* the name it would carry until it was withdrawn. The Castle was used in both directions between Newport and Shrewsbury. 3 July 1983.

STEAM-HAULED SPECIAL TRAINS • 179

243. Jubilee class 4-6-0 5690 *Leander* passes All Stretton with 'The West Mercian' railtour from London St. Pancras. The Jubilee headed the train from Chester to Hereford. Between 1934 and 1936, 191 Jubilee class locomotives were built at Crewe Works, Derby Works, and by the North British Locomotive Company. 28 January 1984.

Opposite above: **244. LMSR Stanier** 4-6-0 5000, built at Crewe in 1935, is one of 842 'Black Five' mixed traffic locomotives built between 1934 and 1951. Here, the locomotive is seen heading north from Craven Arms, near Cheney Longville, with a 'Welsh Marches Pullman'. The train was organised by the Humberside Locomotive Preservation Group. Withdrawn in 1967, 5000 is part of the National Collection. 5 March 1983.

Opposite below: **245. Castle class 4-6-0** 5051 *Drysllwyn Castle* exits Ludlow Tunnel under Gravel Hill, with a southbound 'Welsh Marches Pullman'. The Collett Castle was built at Swindon Works in May 1936 and withdrawn from service in May 1963 when it was sold to Woodham Brothers at Barry. It was the fourth locomotive to be removed from the scrapyard for preservation, and is based at Didcot Railway Centre. 9 April 1983.

STEAM-HAULED SPECIAL TRAINS • 181

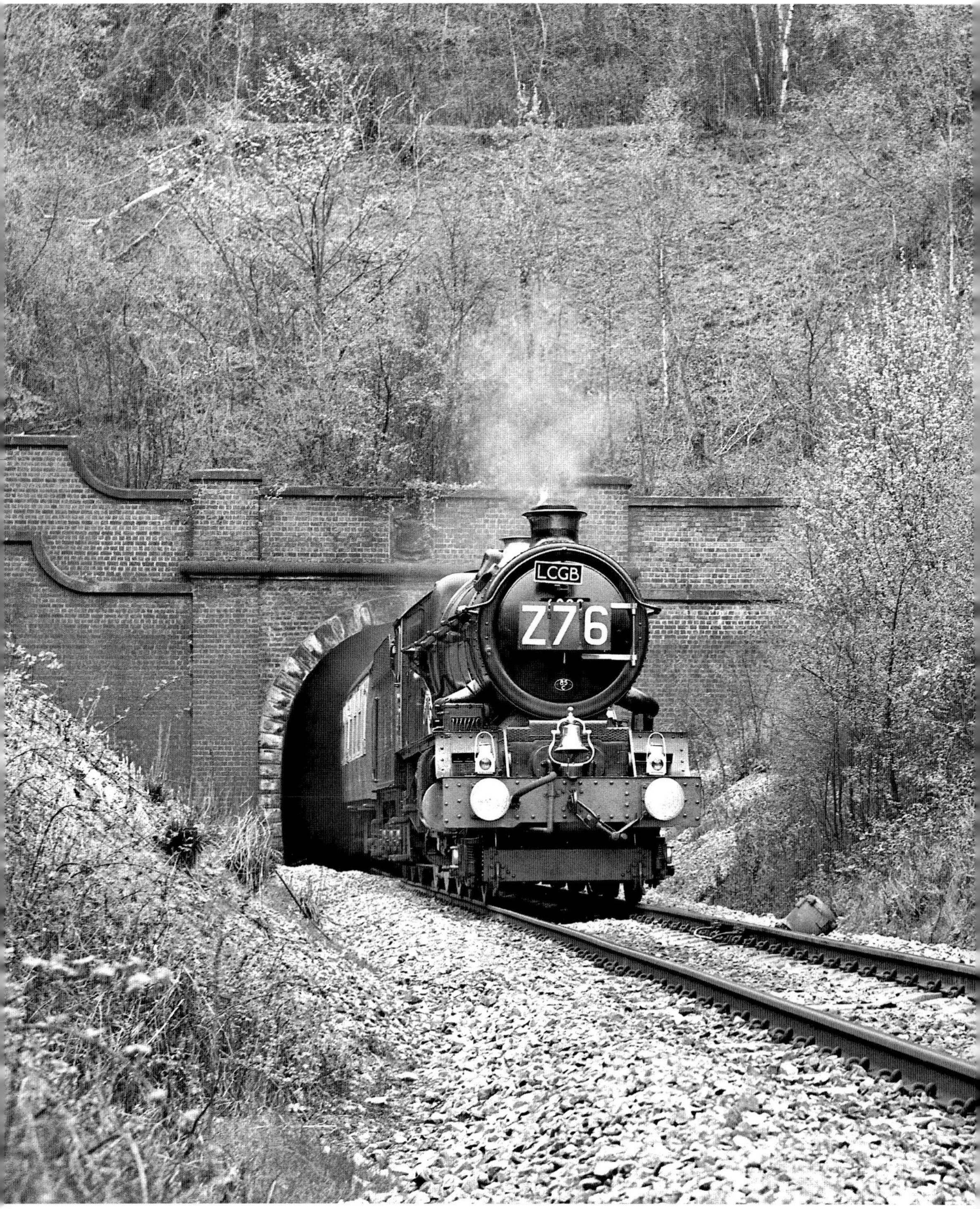
LCGB
Z76

STEAM-HAULED SPECIAL TRAINS • 183

Opposite: **246. The Locomotive** Club of Great Britain's 'The Powisman' railtour emerges from the later of the Dinmore Tunnels behind GWR 4-6-0 6000 *King George V*, as it heads south towards Hereford. The train ran from London Euston to South Wales and the Central Wales line using a variety of motive power. The King headed the train between Shrewsbury and Newport. 20 April 1974.

247. Ivatt Class 4 2-6-0 43106 and GWR Collett 4-6-0 7812 *Erlestoke Manor* pass Brecon Curve junction as they depart from Hereford with the Hereford to Chester leg of the 'Welsh Marches Pullman'. Known as 'The Flying Pig', 43106 was built by BR at Darlington North Road Works in 1951, one of 162 members of the class. Withdrawn in June 1968, the locomotive arrived at the Severn Valley Railway (SVR) in August 1968. *Erlestoke Manor*, built in 1939, is one of thirty Manor class mixed traffic locomotives built between 1938 and 1950. Withdrawn in 1965, 7812 was purchased from Barry Scrapyard by The Erlestoke Manor Fund, departing in May 1974. It is now based at the SVR. 5 June 1982.

Above: **248. In 1968,** cider producer H.P. Bulmer opened a railway centre at their Hereford factory, which was located next to the former Brecon line and so had a connection with British Rail. GWR 6000 *King George V* was leased from Swindon Council and overhauled, ready to form an exhibition train with five Pullman cars. In 1971, the exhibition train ran from Hereford to Tyseley, Birmingham, ending the steam ban on the main line. The centre became home to a number of other locomotives and a base for steam operations on the Welsh Marches line. Here, after heading a 'Welsh Marches Pullman' railtour from Shrewsbury to Hereford, 7812 *Erlestoke Manor* and 4930 *Hagley Hall* stand at Bulmer's Railway Centre. Stanier Pacific 6201 *Princess Elizabeth* is on the left. *Hagley Hall*, built at Swindon in 1929, is a GWR Collett Hall class locomotive. It is one of 258 built between 1928 and 1943. Withdrawn from service in December 1963, it arrived at Barry Scrapyard in May 1964. Purchased for use on the SVR, it reached there in January 1973. 24 April 1982.

Opposite above: **249. Surrounded by** the usual crowd of photographers and onlookers, Stanier 4-6-0 5000 departs from Hereford and heads for Newport with a southbound 'Welsh Marches Pullman'. Stanier Jubilee 4-6-0 5690 *Leander* stands in the station after bringing the train from Shrewsbury. 13 March 1982.

STEAM-HAULED SPECIAL TRAINS • **185**

Below: **250.** **Standard class 4** 4-6-0 75069 passes Meole Brace as it heads away from Shrewsbury with a special train from London Euston to Aberystwyth. Designed by R.A. Riddles, 75069 was built at Swindon in 1955. It was withdrawn eleven years later, in September 1966 and arrived at the SVR, where it is still based, from Barry Scrapyard in March 1973. 22 September 1991.

THE LLANGOLLEN RAILWAY

251. The Llangollen Railway is a standard gauge heritage railway which runs for ten miles between Llangollen and Corwen along the former GWR route from Ruabon to Barmouth Junction, closed in 1965. The railway reopened a short section of track for tourists in 1975 and was extended to Berwyn in 1986, reaching Carrog in 1996. Although most trains on the railway are steam-hauled, diesel traction is also used. Here, class 25/3 25313 arrives at Llangollen with a service from Carrog. Locomotives of this class were known as 'Rats' and this example was one of four that were used on Hertfordshire Railtours' 'Mersey Ratcatcher' railtour from London Euston on 28 September 1986, the last railtour to use class 25 locomotives. 22 October 1994.

THE LLANGOLLEN RAILWAY • **187**

252. Carrying 'The Master Cutler' headboard, class 24 diesel-electric 24081 runs alongside the River Dee, between Carrog and Berwyn, as it heads for Llangollen during a diesel gala on the Llangollen Railway. Now preserved at the Gloucestershire Warwickshire Steam Railway, 24081 was the last member of the class to be withdrawn by BR, in 1980. 19 October 1996.

THE TELFORD STEAM RAILWAY

253. The Telford Steam Railway (TSR), opened in 1984, is a heritage railway at Horsehay, Telford. It operates on the former Wellington and Severn Junction railway between Horsehay & Dawley and Lawley Village, and along a short spur to Spring Village. Here, Peckett 0-4-0ST *Rocket* (1722 of 1926), stands at Spring Village. *Rocket* previously worked at Courtaulds, Coventry. 11 April 2010.

THE TELFORD STEAM RAILWAY • 189

254. At the TSR, a two foot gauge 0-4-0 steam tram, built by Alan Keef Ltd circa 1977, runs around the railway's yard, near Horsehay Pool. The tram, which previously ran along the side of the lake in Telford town park, was moved to the TSR in the mid 1980s. 11 April 2010.

THE SEVERN VALLEY RAILWAY

255. The Severn Valley Railway (SVR) opened in 1862, linking Hartlebury and Shrewsbury. Stations along the line included Bewdley, Arley, Highley, Hampton Loade, and Bridgnorth. It was operated by the West Midland Railway which was later absorbed by the GWR, who opened a line between Bewdley and Kidderminster in 1878. The line was closed to through services in 1963, but coal traffic continued south of Alveley until 1969. Freight between British Sugar Corporation's factory at Foley Park and Kidderminster ended in 1982. In 1967, a new Severn Valley Railway Company was incorporated and, operating as a preserved railway, services commenced in 1970 between Bridgnorth and Hampton Loade, were extended to Bewdley in 1974, and reached Kidderminster in 1984. Here, Ivatt 2MT 2-6-0 46521, built at Swindon in 1953, departs from Bridgnorth station with a train to Bewdley. The locomotive was withdrawn in November 1966 and moved to Barry Scrapyard in March 1967. It arrived at the SVR in March 1971. In total, 128 locomotives of this type were built at Crewe, Darlington and Swindon between 1946 and 1953. 6 July 1975.

THE SEVERN VALLEY RAILWAY • 191

256. The locomotive shed building at Bridgnorth was built using parts of a disused building at Portskewett, near Severn Tunnel Junction. Construction started in March 1976 and was completed in April 1977. Later that year, Hawksworth Modified Hall 4-6-0 6960 *Raveningham Hall*, built at Swindon in 1944, stands outside the shed. Fowler 'Jinty' 3F 0-6-0T 47383, built at the Vulcan Foundry for the LMSR in 1926, is on the right, with Manning Wardle 0-6-0ST (2047 of 1926) *Warwickshire* on the left. *Raveningham Hall* was moved from Barry Scrapyard in October 1972, 47383 arrived from Blackwell 'A' Winning Colliery in May 1968, and *Warwickshire* was purchased from Rugby Portland Cement in October 1967. 18 June 1977.

257. Riddles 2-10-0 600 *Gordon* and British Railways Standard Class 4 2-6-4T 80079 head away from Bridgnorth and approach Oldbury Viaduct with a train to Bewdley. *Gordon* was built by the North British Locomotive Company (25437 of 1943) and is a Second World War Austerity locomotive. It arrived at the SVR from the Longmoor Military Railway in September 1971. Standard tank engine 80079, built in 1954 at Brighton, was withdrawn in July 1965. It arrived at the SVR from Barry Scrapyard in May 1971. 23 April 1983.

Opposite above: **258. Ivatt Class** 4 43106 2-6-0 43106 drifts down Eardington Bank towards Eardington Halt with a Bridgnorth to Bewdley service. The telegraph poles were later removed. 9 October 1977.

Opposite below: **259. Class 52 D1062** *Western Courier* passes Eardington Halt and heads for Kidderminster with a train from Bridgnorth. W*estern Courier* is a type 4 C-C diesel-hydraulic locomotive, built at Crewe in 1963, one of seventy-four 'Westerns' built between 1961 and 1964 for BR (Western Region). D1062 was bought from BR by the Western Locomotive Association in 1976 and was the first 'Western' to be preserved. The boiler of GWR pannier tank 3612 is on the platform. The locomotive was purchased for spares from Barry Scrapyard in 1978. 9 May 1990.

THE SEVERN VALLEY RAILWAY • 193

Above: **260. GWR 3700** class 4-4-0 3440 *City of Truro,* renumbered 3717 in 1912, runs alongside Northwood Lane and approaches Bewdley, as it heads for Kidderminster. The location is the former junction of the Tenbury line and the area on the left is the trackbed of the line to Tenbury, which once continued to Woofferton. The locomotive, visiting the SVR for the Autumn Gala in 1991, was built at Swindon in 1903 to the design of George Jackson Churchward, and is considered by some to be the first steam locomotive to reach 100 miles per hour, in 1904. 22 September 1991.

Opposite above: **261. With the** trackbed of the former Tenbury line on the right, Ivatt 2MT 2-6-0 46443 heads north from Bewdley. Built at Crewe in 1950, it was withdrawn in March 1967. Purchased from BR, it arrived at the SVR in the April of that year. The locomotive was one of four used on the SVR during the filming of Universal Pictures' *Seven-Per-Cent Solution*, released in 1976. It is seen here, numbered 60 116 and painted in Furness Railway red, with a flared stovepipe chimney and a large brass dome added, to represent an Austrian Railways locomotive. 26 October 1975.

Opposite below: **262. Class 25/3** diesel-electrics 25303 and 25258 are pictured at Bewdley with the Great Western Society's 'The John Mynors Memorial Train'. The special train ran from Paddington to Dorridge behind GWR Castle class 4-6-0 5051 *Drysllwyn Castle*. The class 25/3s then took it on to Bewdley, where the SVR's GWR 2-8-0 2857 took over for the run to Bridgnorth. 14 September 1980.

THE SEVERN VALLEY RAILWAY • 195

263. Built by the SVR on the site of Comberton Hill Goods Yard, Kidderminster Town station is based on the GWR station at Ross-On-Wye. Here, soon after opening and before the construction of the station building and signal box, GWR Collett 4-6-0 4930 *Hagley Hall* departs from Kidderminster Town with a train to Bridgnorth. The old GWR goods shed and water tower are on the right. SVR trains can access the BR line at Kidderminster. 5 August 1984.

THE WELSHPOOL AND LLANFAIR LIGHT RAILWAY

264. The Welshpool & Llanfair Light Railway (W&LLR) is a 2ft 6in gauge narrow gauge railway running 8½ miles from Welshpool to Llanfair Caereinion. Opened in 1903, the railway was closed by British Railways in 1956 and reopened as a heritage railway in 1963. Originally it ran from a station next to the standard gauge line in Welshpool, but now starts from a station at Raven Square on the edge of the town. Two locomotives were built for the line by Beyer Peacock in 1902 and were stored at Oswestry Works after the railway closed. Here, 823 *Countess*, the second of the original locomotives, heads a short train to Llanfair Caereinion, made up of two replica Pickering coaches, away from the new station at Raven Square. 10 August 2008.

265. The terminus of the W&LLR is at Llanfair Caereinion. Here, 14, former Sierra Leone Government Railway 2-6-2T 85, built by the Hunslet Engine Company (3815 of 1954), shunts passenger stock at Llanfair Caereinion station. The locomotive arrived at the W&LLR in 1975. 25 August 1980.

OTHER RECENT PRESERVATION PROJECTS

Cambrian Heritage Railways

266. Trains run from Oswestry, for 1¾ miles through the suburbs of Oswestry, to a new station at Weston Wharf. It is the intention to extend the line to Llynclys South, five miles south of Oswestry on the former Cambrian Railway line which previously served Blodwell Quarry. Here, with Oswestry station building and signal box in the background, Andrew Barclay 0-4-0ST *Henry Ellison* (2217 of 1947) departs from Oswestry with a train to Weston Wharf. 3 April 2022.

The Glyn Valley Tramway

267. The 2 foot 4½ inch gauge Glyn Valley Tramway ran for 8¼ miles from Chirk to Glyn Ceirog. Passenger services ended in 1933 and the line was closed in 1935. The Glyn Valley Tramway Trust has commenced work on the restoration of the line and here the trackbed and the platform of the old railway can once more be seen next to Chirk main line station. 3 April 2022.

Finally

268. The loop signals are at danger in both directions on this unusual signal post in Coton Hill Yard, Shrewsbury. 30 January 1988.

BIBLIOGRAPHY

Baker, S. K., *Rail Atlas Great Britain and Ireland*, (Haynes Publishing Group, 1980 and 1988)

British Rail, *British Rail Passenger Timetable(s)*, May 1984-October 1993, (British Railways Board, 1984-1993)

British Railways Pre-Grouping Atlas and Gazetteer, (Ian Allan Publishing Ltd, 1980)

Gradients of the British Main Line Railways, (Ian Allan Publishing Ltd, 2016)

Jowett, A., *Jowett's Railway Atlas of Great Britain and Ireland*, (Patrick Stephens Ltd, 1989)

Marsden, C., *35 Years of Main Line Diesel Traction*, (Oxford Publishing Co., 1982)

Rhodes, M. and Shannon, P., *Freight Only Volume 2: Southern and Central England*, (Silver Link 1988)

Rhodes, M. and Shannon, P., *Freight Only Volume 3: Wales and Scotland*, (Silver Link 1988)

Signalling Study Group, *The Signal Box, A Pictorial History*, (Oxford Publishing Co., 1986)

Wood, R., *British Rail Locomotives*, (Ian Allan Ltd, 1986)

INDEX TO LOCATIONS BY PHOTO NUMBER

Albrighton, 144
All Stretton, 181, 242-243
Allscott, 115-116

Baschurch, 30, 236
Bayston Hill, 174-176
Bersham Colliery, 54, 239
Bewdley, 260-262
Blodwell Quarry, 40, 42
Bridgnorth, 255-257
Bromfield, 208-209
Bucknell, 200

Carrog, 252
Cefn Mawr Viaduct, 50
Cefn-y-Bedd, 60
Cheney Longville, 193, 244
Chester, 67-73
Chirk, 48-49, 267
Church Stretton, 182-186
Coalbrookdale, 134-136
Codsall1, 45-148
Condover, 240
Cosford, 140-143
Craven Arms, 192, 194-197
Crewe, 102-105

Dinmore Tunnels, 224, 246
Dorrington, 177-180, 241

Eardington, 258-259

Ford Bridge, 221-223

Gobowen, 34-36, 43-45

Harlescott, 83
Haughton Sidings, 31-32
Hawarden Bridge, 63
Hereford, 226-234, 247-249
Hookagate, 162
Hopton Heath, 198-199
Horsehay, 254

Ironbridge, 137

Kidderminster, 263
Knighton, 202-204

Leaton, 29
Leominster, 217-220
Lightmoor Junction, 132-133
Little Stretton, 187-188
Llanfair Caereinion, 265
Llangollen, 251
Ludlow, 210-212, 245

Madeley Junction, 131, 138
Marshbrook, 189-190
Meole Brace, 160-161, 250
Moreton-on-Lugg, 225

Nantwich, 100-101

Oakengates, 130
Onibury, 206-207
Oswestry, 37-39, 266
Oxley, 149

Penyffordd, 61
Porthywaen, 41
Prees, 90

Rossett, 65-66
Ruabon, 51-53, 238

Shifnal, 139
Shotton, 62
Shrewsbury, 1-28, 74-82, 106-109, 153-159, 170-173, 235, 268
Spring Village, 253
Stafford Junction, Wellington, 124-126
Stokesay, 205
Stowe, 201

Telford Central, 129
Trench Crossing, 127-128

Upton Magna, 110-111

Walcot, 112-115
Wellington, 117-123
Welshpool, 166-169, 264
Wem, 86-89
Westbury, 163-165
Weston Rhyn, 46-47
Whitchurch, 91-95
Whittington, 33
Wistanstow, 191
Wolverhampton, 150-152
Woofferton, 213-216
Wrenbury, 96-99
Wrexham, 55-59, 64, 237

Yorton, 84-85